Lakota Recollections
of the Custer Fight

NEW SOURCES OF
INDIAN-MILITARY HISTORY

compiled and edited by
RICHARD G. HARDORFF

Introduction to the Bison Books Edition by
JEROME A. GREENE

University of Nebraska Press
Lincoln and London

♾ The paper in this book meets the minimum requirements of American
National Standard for Information Sciences—Permanence of Paper for
Printed Library Materials, ANSI Z39.48-1984.

First Bison Books printing: 1997

Library of Congress Cataloging-in-Publication Data
Lakota recollections of the Custer fight: new sources of Indian-military
history / compiled and edited by Richard G. Hardorff; introduction to the
Bison Books edition by Jerome A. Greene.
p.   cm.
Originally published: Spokane, Wash.: A. H. Clarke Co., 1991.
Includes bibliographical references and index.
ISBN 0-8032-7293-6 (pbk.: alk. paper)
1. Little Bighorn, Battle of the, Mont., 1876—Personal narratives.
2. Dakota Indians—Interviews.   3. Dakota Indians—Wars, 1876.
4. Dakota Indians—Biography.   I. Hardorff, Richard G.
E83.876.L27   1997
973.8'2—dc21
96-46297   CIP

Reprinted from the original 1991 edition by the Arthur H. Clark Company,
Spokane, Washington.

That which is good in this work
is dedicated to the memory of
JUDGE ELI S. RICKER

Contents

Illustrations

Maps

Introduction

Jerome A. Greene

When historian and retired army colonel William A. Graham introduced a selection of Indian recollections of the Battle of the Little Big Horn in his 1953 book, *The Custer Myth*, he admonished his audience: "The reader will find in these Indian statements discrepancies and contradictions and inconsistencies. He will have to do with them as all who have studied them have done, and reconcile them if and as he can."[1] Graham's statement succinctly assessed the essence of the era's perception of Indian testimony about the Little Big Horn—that as a body it lacked sufficient credibility and consistency to win serious acceptance within the history community. (Who knows how much latent racial intolerance colored this perception?) Despite his own criticism, Graham presented in his book the most comprehensive collection to that time of Lakota (Sioux), Northern Cheyenne, Crow, and Arikara personal recollections about how the battle started, progressed, and ended.[2]

As tendered by Graham (although available separately through other publications prior to 1953), the accounts of the Crows and Arikaras who had served the army as scouts in 1876 were useful because they added to the knowledge of Major Reno's opening action in the Little Big Horn Valley and his subsequent withdrawal to the bluffs east of and overlooking the river. The Crow testimony was additionally significant because it addressed part of Custer's route and the beginning of his battalion's engagement as it sought to ford the Little Big Horn River nearly three miles from the action of Reno's command. But most Crow and Arikara statements merely augmented the known record of the Reno-Benteen action. The Sioux and Cheyenne recollections did likewise, but they added a unique and important dimension in explaining the defeat of Custer's battalion—that phase of the Battle of the Little Big Horn from which no soldier eyewitnesses escaped.

Curiosity about what happened to Custer's command has been paramount almost since the event occurred 120 years ago. It is just as compelling today. For, of the hundreds of clashes between troops and Indians in the trans-Mississippi West between 1865 and 1891, only that at the Little Big Horn has captured public imagination and has come to symbolize them all. Astoundingly, a major segment of the Seventh U.S. Cavalry Regiment was obliterated. The potential value of Indian participant descriptions in explaining what happened during Custer's phase of the engagement was obvious.

The quest for answers became especially pronounced in the weeks and months following the Little Big Horn debacle, as it became apparent that Indian accounts of the battle held possible explanations for Custer's demise. It was not, however, until late in 1876 and early in 1877 that the first sketchy Indian reports surfaced from among tribesmen turning themselves in at agencies in Nebraska and Dakota Territory. These accounts, together with those rendered in subsequent years through the early 1880s, comprise what might accurately be termed *immediate testimony*, that is statements given within months or, at the most, a few years after the event. Presumably tainted by faulty language translation, often contaminated by an interviewer's bias, and otherwise sensationalized by a news correspondent's prose, the immediate accounts, though of potentially valuable content, posed a jumble of contradictory statements that confused and deepened the mystery of Custer's last hours. Additional Sioux narratives became available in 1881, following the return and surrender of Sitting Bull's people from their self-imposed exile in Canada since the closing operations of the Great Sioux War. But like the earlier ones, the accounts of the early 1880s either were muddled by the presence of cultural and linguistic subtleties incomprehensible to most whites or they betrayed the interviewer's anticipaton of retribution. In sum, these Indian accounts offered little to explain the tactical intricacies of the Custer fight.[3] As a result, early Indian reminiscences about the Little Big Horn, despite whatever truth they contained, were deemed irreconcilable and of little value in comprehending the event. Seventy years later, when Graham published several of the early Sioux and Cheyenne accounts, he submitted them for the purpose of interest alone, dismissing them as barely plausible ingredients in unraveling the mystery of Custer's defeat.

Whatever credibility gaps might have lingered from the existence of the earliest native renderings, within two decades a second wave of Indian reflections appeared, largely inspired and generated by a corps of insightful individuals motivated by the singular purpose of getting at the truth. These were drawn from among the veteran warriors who had participated in the fighting at the Little Big Horn and had been present during Custer's battle. This body of recollections, whether elicited by professional scholars or by knowledgeable students of the battle, comprises salient *reminiscent testimony* and is represented in the work of such persons as Eli S. Ricker, Walter M. Camp, and George Bird Grinnell. All were qualified and skilled interrogators; all kept detailed records of their interviews with the former combatants (and noncombatants, as well). The work of Ricker, Camp, Grinnell, and others in recording important recollections and in constantly cross-checking the results of their dialogue against other accounts during interviews conducted from the 1890s into the early 1920s produced the most comprehensive and conclusive collection of Indian statements known regarding the Battle of the Little Big Horn.[4] Although reminiscent testimony might be criticized as being too distantly removed from the events and thus based upon too-vague memories, it perhaps more importantly afforded interviewees a temporal detachment and an objectivity that the early recountants, influenced by real or imagined reprisal for their presence at the Little Big Horn, could never attain.[5]

Between the 1920s and 1950s yet another body of reminiscent data from Indian participants emerged through the efforts of such students as Dr. Thomas B. Marquis, Eleanor H. Hinman, John G. Neihardt, Stanley Vestal (Walter S. Campbell), and even Mari Sandoz, who used many of the Hinman transcripts in her book *Crazy Horse*, published in 1942. Many of these Indian statements offered new perspectives not only of the Little Big Horn but of other period army-Indian engagements, as well.[6] But as more and more time passed, increasingly clouded memories made additional Indian contributions noted more for their sheer antiquity than for their value of content. By the late 1950s and early 1960s, reminiscent testimony came from the aged descendants of the Little Big Horn battle participants. Their assertions, while of possible corroborative value, nevertheless constituted hearsay.[7] Although this second-hand information proved interesting in cogitating over what had happened on Custer's field nearly a century before, it was decidedly not as significant as that from persons who actively took part in the action there.

While evincing some of the typical liabilities associated with the earliest Indian testimony, the reminiscent accounts nonetheless afford the only major participant evidence that might reasonably explain the destruction of Custer's five cavalry companies of cavalry on the afternoon of 25 June 1876. Furthermore, much of its value has been confirmed by modern archaeological investigation of the battlefield during the 1980s and 1990s.[8] Studied comparatively against the early testimony, the reminiscent narratives, coupled with data results of the archaeology, have brought renewed regard for the Sioux and Cheyenne recollections in terms of their veracity of content. They have consequently gained enhanced importance in promoting interpretations about key developments in the maneuvering of the cavalry and Indian forces on the battlefield.[9] Taken together, the Indian accounts almost universally portray one or more of four conspicuous movements of Custer's battalion, or parts of it, as follows: (1) the occurrence of a confrontation between troops and Indians at the ford of the Little Big Horn River at the mouth of what is today called Medicine Tail Coulee; (2) the diagonal withdrawal of a military force back from the ford and toward the hogback "battle" ridge along which many soldiers perished and where the so-called last stand took place; (3) an action along the southeast end of the battle ridge known as "Calhoun Hill"; and, late in the fighting, (4) the final rush of surviving soldiers from their open position on the battle ridge down toward the tree-lined riverbank where they might find cover.

With their uniquely personalized character, the accounts contained in this book notably ratify the above scenarios while offering others, thus adding significantly to the body of extant Indian testimony about the Little Big Horn. As well, they represent some of the best examples of reminiscent testimony from the turn of the century forward. Richard G. Hardorff introduces an impressive array of recollections from fourteen Lakotas, one Northern Cheyenne, and a white interpreter with knowledge derived from interviewing many of the tribesmen about the battle. In each instance, biographical data about the recountant helps establish his or her association with the Little Big Horn and often includes the circumstances under which the individual came to be interviewed. Further, Hardorff's learned assessment of the accounts and his comparison of them to those of other participants (as well as to extant accounts by the same subject) afford readers more knowledge of the entire spectrum of Indian testimony regarding the Custer fight. The information is refreshingly new and exciting, deeply personal, and historically important in establishing new dimensions about one of the most dramatic and controversial episodes in American frontier history.

NOTES

1. William A. Graham, comp., *The Custer Myth: A Source Book of Custeriana* (Harrisburg PA: The Stackpole Company, 1953), 4.

2. The Battle of the Little Big Horn, 25–26 June 1876, consisted of three primary actions: Major Marcus A. Reno's attack on, and subsequent retreat from, the south end of the combined Sioux-Cheyenne village in Little Big Horn Valley; Lieutenant Colonel George A. Custer's battle on the ridges above the river three-to-four miles north of Reno, in which engagement his entire battalion perished; and the fight of Reno's and Captain Frederick W. Benteen's combined commands on the bluffs east of the river through the afternoon and evening of the 25th and through the day of the 26th until the warriors finally left the area.

3. For discussion of the numerous problems inherent in Indian testimony, see Jerome A. Greene, "The Uses of Indian Testimony in the Writing of Indian Wars History," *Order of the Indian Wars Journal*, 2 (winter 1981): 2–3; and Jerome A. Greene, "The Great Sioux War and Indian Testimony," in Greene, comp., *Lakota and Cheyenne: Indian Views of the Great Sioux War, 1876–1877* (Norman: University of Oklahoma Press, 1994), xxi–xxii.

4. Ricker's materials are in seventeen boxes of manuscripts housed at the Nebraska State Historical Society, Lincoln. Much of the Ricker materials is available on microfilm through the society. Camp's manuscripts are in the special collection repositories at Indiana University, Bloomington; the Denver Public Library; Brigham Young University, Provo, Utah; and Little Bighorn Battlefield National Monument, Crow Agency, Montana. Most, if not all, are available on microfilm through the Brigham Young University venue. Grinnell's papers, including his interviews, are in the manuscript holdings of the Southwest Museum, Los Angeles. See also the Joseph G. Masters Papers (also on microfilm), Kansas State Historical Society, Topeka, for interviews by this contemporary of

Camp and Ricker. Selected items from the Camp, Ricker, and Grinnell interviews have been variously published. See, for example, Walter M. Camp, *Custer in '76: Walter Camp's Notes on the Custer Fight,* ed. Kenneth M. Hammer (Provo: Brigham Young University Press, 1976); Greene, *Lakota and Cheyenne;* and Richard G. Hardorff, comp., *Cheyenne Memories of the Custer Fight: A Source Book* (Spokane: Arthur H. Clark Company, 1995).

5. Regarding the value of Indian testimony, "the seemingly disparate accounts of Indian combatants offer, in many ways, data that intersect on points basic to the consideration of a particular battle action. In this respect, the treatment of Indian eyewitness reports proceeds much like that of other accounts. Whereas a single observer may be sufficient, additional statements by other independent witnesses, compared point for point, might enhance the credibility of all." Greene, "The Uses of Indian Testimony," 3. See also Greene, "Great Sioux War and Indian Testimony," xxii–xxiii.

6. See, for example, Thomas B. Marquis, *A Warrior Who Fought Custer* (Minneapolis: Midwest Company, 1931; reprinted as *Wooden Leg* [Lincoln: University of Nebraska Press, 1957]); Thomas B. Marquis, *She Watched Custer's Last Battle* (Hardin MT: privately printed, 1933); Thomas B. Marquis, *Which Indian Killed Custer* (Hardin MT: privately printed, 1933); "Oglala Sources on the Life of Crazy Horse. Interviews Given to Eleanor H. Hinman," *Nebraska History,* 57 (spring 1976): 1–46; John G. Neihardt, *Black Elk Speaks: Being the Life Story of a Holy Man of the Oglala Sioux* (Lincoln: University of Nebraska Press, 1961); Stanley Vestal, *New Sources of Indian History, 1850–1891* (Norman: University of Oklahoma Press, 1934); Stanley Vestal, *Warpath: The True Story of the Fighting Sioux Told in a Biography of Chief White Bull* (Boston: Houghton Mifflin, 1934); Stanley Vestal, "The Man Who Killed Custer," *American Heritage,* 8 (February 1957): 4–9, 90–91; and Mari Sandoz, *Crazy Horse, The Strange Man of the Oglalas* (New York: Hastings House, 1942). Transcripts of Vestal's interviews with Indians are in the Western History Collections of the University of Oklahoma Library.

7. The best example is John Stands in Timber and Margot Liberty, *Cheyenne Memories* (New Haven: Yale University Press, 1967).

8. See Douglas D. Scott and Richard A. Fox, Jr., *Archaeological Insights into the Custer Battle: An Assessment of the 1984 Field Season* (Norman: University of Oklahoma Press, 1987); Douglas D. Scott, Richard A. Fox Jr., Melissa A. Connor, and Dick Harmon, *Archeological Perspectives on the Battle of the Little Bighorn* (Norman: University of Oklahoma Press, 1989).

9. Examples of the synthetic use of Lakota and Cheyenne recollections in juxtaposition with archaeological data for interpreting the progress of the Custer fight at the Little Big Horn are in Jerome A. Greene, *Evidence and the Custer Enigma,* rev. ed. (Golden CO: Outbooks, 1986); and Richard G. Hardorff, *Markers, Artifacts, and Indian Testimony: Preliminary Findings on the Custer Battle* (Short Hills

NJ: W. D. Horn, 1985). The most comprehensive synthesis to date is Richard Allan Fox Jr., *Archeology, History, and Custer's Last Battle* (Norman: University of Oklahoma Press, 1993). But see also Gregory Michno, *The Mystery of E Troop: The Gray Horse Company at the Little Bighorn* (Missoula MT: Mountain Press Publishing, 1994).

Preface

This publication presents the obscure recollections of eight Oglalas, three Minneconjous, two Hunkpapas, two Brules and, in contradiction with this volume's title, that of one Cheyenne. The interviews were held by men who were genuinely interested in the historical truth. Scholars will recognize such names as Judge Eli S. Ricker, Gen. Hugh L. Scott, Judge Frank Zahn, Dr. John G. Neihardt, and Walter Mason Camp. The recollections obtained by these men provide answers to some of the most perplexing questions which have confronted students of the Custer Battle. It is hoped, therefore, that the publication of these interviews will stimulate the further research on one of the most colorful episodes in American History.

No armed confrontation with American Indians has received as much attention by historians as has the Battle of the Little Bighorn. Fought on Sunday afternoon, June 25, 1876, it resulted in the complete destruction of Lt. Col. George A. Custer and five companies of the Seventh U.S. Cavalry by Sioux and Cheyenne Indians.

News of the disaster shocked a nation which was then in the midst of celebrating its first centennial accomplishments. And even after the passing of more than a century, the interest in this relatively insignificant confrontation has not waned, but instead, it continues to speak to the imagination of the American people. Most of this continuing popular appeal can be accounted for because of the impact of the tragedy—Custer and his entire command were wiped out, including two of his brothers, one brother-in-law, and a nephew who fell with him that Sunday; and also because people are still drawn to Custer's own illustrious and flamboyant personality and controversial career which he built during the Civil War where he reached the rank of brevet Major General.

The seeds for the Custer tragedy were sown as far back as 1868. In that year, the Treaty of Fort Laramie granted to the Sioux and Cheyenne Indians the Black Hills area "as long as the grass was green and the sky was blue." But before the ink was barely dry, gold was discovered in the Black Hills. A geological expedition in 1874 confirmed the existence of the precious ore causing a rush of fortune hunters onto the Indian lands.

Attempts by the Army to turn back the hordes of encroaching whites failed as did an attempt by the U.S. Government to buy the Black Hills from the Indians. Emotions between both sides escalated. The Sioux charged the U.S. Government with breaking the Laramie Treaty by allowing white encroachment. The whites, however, made counter charges that the Sioux and Cheyennes were raiding settlements and travel routes adjacent to the Indian lands.

Frustrated by the Indian situation, the Indian Bureau issued an ultimatum to all Indians on the unceded hunting grounds: either immediately return to the reservation, or be classified as hostiles after January 31, 1876. When this deadline passed, the matter was turned over to the War Department for military action.

Early in 1876, a three-pronged campaign was launched to force the Sioux and Cheyennes back onto their reservations. The Montana Column, commanded by Col. John Gibbon, marched east from Fort Ellis, near present Bozeman, Montana. The Dakota Column was led by Gen. Alfred H. Terry. It included Lt. Col. George A. Custer and the Seventh U.S. Cavalry, which headed west from Fort Lincoln, near present Bismarck, North Dakota. These two columns were to join on the Yellowstone River. The third column departed from Fort Fetterman, near present Sheridan, Wyoming. It was commanded by Gen. George Crook and moved north into Montana. These three units, totalling nearly 3000 men, were to meet in the vicinity of the Little Bighorn near the end of June.

In March of 1876, a military strike force from Crook's column under Col. J.J. Reynolds surprised a winter camp of Cheyennes on the Powder River. The Indians rallied, however, and staged a counter attack, forcing Reynolds to abandon the field and to retreat to Crook's main column. Rumors abounded that Reynolds had bungled the affair, which later led to his courtmartial.

On June 17, Gen. George Crook's column of 1300 men was caught by surprise on Rosebud Creek by a large force of Sioux and Cheyenne Indians. This day-long battle caused surprisingly few casualties on either side. It did result, however, in Crook's withdrawal from the battlefield. He returned to his supply camp to await reinforcements, thereby ceasing to be any further threat to the Indians.

After joining with Col. Gibbon's column on the Yellowstone, the Seventh Cavalry was dispatched on June 22, to find and engage the hostiles. Custer's column consisted of 31 officers, 585 enlisted men, 40 U.S. Indian Scouts, and some 20 packers, guides, and other civilian employees. The regiment marched up the Rosebud, and on June 24, it made bivouac near the present town of Busby, Montana.

On the evening of June 24, Custer decided to leave the valley and follow the trail of the Indians which led west, across the Wolf Mountains, into the valley of the Little Bighorn. Accordingly, the regiment commenced a night march so as to cross the mountains before dawn to prevent discovery by the hostiles. However, the darkness and difficulties with the pack train did not allow the regiment to cover much distance during the night. As a result, the march came to a halt at daylight, several miles short of the divide.

On the early morning of June 25, U.S. Indian Scouts confirmed the existence of a large Indian village in the Little Bighorn Valley. Custer was notified of this observation, but he himself was unable to discern anything from a rocky promontory on the divide. In the meantime, the regiment was discovered by several Indian parties which passed in the vicinity. Since concealment now no longer served any purpose, the decision was made to advance on the village immediately.

At noon on June 25, the cavalry crossed the divide of the Wolf Mountains. From this vantage point, dust clouds were seen hanging over the Little Bighorn Valley, some thirteen miles to the west. In compliance with Gen. Terry's instructions not to let the Indians escape to the south, Custer dispatched Capt. Frederick W. Benteen with companies D, H, and K in a southwesterly direction. Benteen was to march toward a line of bluffs and from there ascertain that the Indians were not fleeing up the Little Bighorn. If any Indians were sighted, Benteen was to commence a holding action and was to notify Custer at once.

The remaining nine companies were divided into three

battalions. One battalion was commanded by Major Marcus A. Reno, which consisted of Companies A, M, and G. Capt. Myles W. Keogh was given command of Companies C, I, and L, while Capt. George F. Yates received command of Companies E and F. Company B, commanded by Capt. Thomas M. McDougall, was detailed to escort the pack train, which force was further augmented by seven troopers from each company.

After dispatching Capt. Benteen to the southwest, the balance of the regiment continued to follow the winding course of Reno Creek. Near the lower forks—some four miles east of the Little Bighorn—they came across a deserted Indian village in which a single funeral lodge was standing. The telltale signs of rising smoke from burning fire pits, and abandoned household goods indicated clearly to all that this village site was hastily vacated.

The sight of this deserted village must have added considerably to Custer's apprehension that the hostiles had begun to scatter. This impression was reinforced moments later when he was told of a band of Indians seen fleeing on ponies over a rise near the river. Accordingly, Major Reno was given instructions to take his battalion and pursue the hostiles—to commence a holding action until the balance of the regiment arrived to support him.

After crossing to the west bank of the river, it soon became clear to Major Reno that the Indians were not fleeing at all, and that the troops had struck a village of enormous size. Reno therefore discarded his order of a vigorous charge and halted his battalion to form a dismounted skirmish line. This line extended some two hundred yards across the valley floor, its right flank resting perpendicular on a dry river bend, just south of present Garryowen, Montana. Here the battle of the Little Bighorn commenced.

Increasing boldness and firepower by the opposing

Indian force soon caused the collapse of this skirmish line, which consequently fell back to the protection of the timber along the bend. Shortly thereafter, Major Reno decided that his position in the woods was no longer tenable and ordered a charge to the bluffs across the river. This charge resulted in the death of some thirty-five men of Reno's battalion.

Having gained the relative security of the bluffs, Reno's troops were soon joined by Capt. Benteen's battalion, which had received written orders to "be quick." Since these orders did not specify that he was to join Custer's command, Capt. Benteen remained with Major Reno's disorganized battalion. In the meantime volley firing was heard which reverberations came from downstream. However, as a result of the many wounded and the fact that the pack train with Capt. McDougall had not arrived as yet, the combined battalions remained inactive on Reno Hill.

Impatient from all the delays, one of Benteen's officers, Capt. Thomas B. Weir, moved his company down the river about a mile, toward the sound of combat. From a vantage point now known as Weir Point, the troops were able to view the present area of Custer Battlefield. Through the rising dust and powder smoke, they saw glimpses of Indians galloping over the field while shooting at objects laying on the ground.

Capt. Weir was soon joined by the balance of the regiment. Apparently, these movements had been observed by the Indians because soon many hostiles were seen to converge onto Weir Point. Since both Reno and Benteen judged the present location inadequate for defense, the regiment was turned around and ordered to fall back to Reno Hill, where they eventually entrenched.

For two days, the troops withstood the Indians and

fought against fatigue and apprehension. One officer keenly observed that during this nightmare in the scorching sun, "young boys soon became old men, and men lay in trench[es] beside corpses with flies and maggots, and struck and fought like old veterans of years' standing." This hell ended on June 27, when Gen. Alfred H. Terry and Col. John Gibbon's Montana Column arrived. The Seventh's survivors then learned of the horrible fate of Custer and his five companies.

How Custer's command perished can not be determined with certainty because no member of it survived. From the placement of strewn bodies and combat refuse, the movements of his two battalions can be roughly reconstructed. But the details of the action, and the factors which shaped them, are bound to remain forever a mystery.

After dispatching Major Reno's battalion to the front, Custer watered his horses and then followed at a slower pace in the rear. Although Major Reno would naturally expect that Custer would follow him into battle by crossing the river, it appears that just before the stream was reached, Custer's attention was directed toward a party of mounted Indians on Reno Hill. Instead of crossing the river, therefore, Custer diverged to the north and arrived on the steep bluffs which border the river on the east side. From this vantage point, Custer's men beheld an enormous Indian village which stretched along the river as far as vision would allow. Below, in the valley, Reno's battalion was seen advancing towards the southern end.

From this location, a sergeant was dispatched with oral orders for both Capt. Benteen and the packtrain to hurry. After following the bluffs for about a mile, the five companies entered present Cedar Coulee, which runs behind the bluffs and parallel with the river. Midway down this coulee a trumpeter was dispatched with a message for Capt. Benteen that a big Indian village was found, and that he, Benteen, was to bring the packs, and to hurry.

While galloping away with his dispatch, Trumpeter John Martin caught a fleeting glimpse of Custer and the dust-caked troopers. This parting glance was the last ever of the five companies alive. Two days later, members of Gibbon's Montana Column found the mutilated corpses clustered in four groups on the battlefield. The bodies of C and L troopers were found strewn along Calhoun Ridge. Half a mile north from here, I Company was annihilated en masse in a little valley. A short distance to the west, on Custer Hill, some 40 men had fallen around Custer, among which were most of the officers, while near the river, twenty-eight bodies were found on the bottom of a deep ravine.

Although the Custer Battle ended on that bloody Sunday a century ago, controversy rages on about Custer's strategy; the movements of his troops; and the order in which the companies were defeated. Speculation continues about such questions as to whether any or all of Custer's five companies went to Medicine Tail Ford, or whether the entire command marched together over Nye-Cartwright Ridge to the battlefield. Was Last Stand Hill indeed the location of the "Last Stand," or does this distinction belong to the defenders of Calhoun Hill? Did the twenty-eight men found on the bottom of Deep Ravine die here while on the skirmish line at the beginning of the fight, or were they fleeing from Custer Hill at the end of the battle? And did the doomed troopers resort to mass suicides? These are but a few of the questions which continue to baffle both the scholar and the historian.

Evidence upon which to base any conclusions is inadequate. As a result, therefore, this entire matter is now clothed in such a mass of supposition and theory that it is nearly impossible to separate the meager facts from the mass of conjecture. There exists, of course, an abundance of information accumulated through diaries, letters, orders and newspapers, but all of these sources contain impressions by individuals who viewed the field *after* the battle. There is, however, an untapped source which has been generally misunderstood and disregarded by many scholars. These are the accounts by Indian combatants, who were the only true eyewitnesses to the Custer Battle.

In order to properly evaluate Indian eyewitness statements, a brief discussion as to the value aspects might be in order. Keeping in mind that statements by Indian informants were given in a language alien to the interrogator, the employment of an interpreter was imperative. Thus, the success of each interview was based on the combined efforts of three people. However, this filtering process produced various results. At worst—which was more often the case than not—the outcome was subject to the informant's distortions, the translator's improficiencies in the Indian language, and the interrogator's lack of objectivity.

Examination of translated Indian accounts reveals in a number of cases that the interrogator had preconceived ideas of the battle. Ignoring the need for historical accuracy, he modified the information through an editing process which called for sensational results. Then, too, the efficiency of the interpreter played a large part in the outcome. His efficiency was based on the ability to understand the cultural background of the Indian, and the proficiency to convey the finer nuances from one language to another. Since most interpreters were barely proficient in the use of English, one cannot help but wonder about the accuracy of their recorded translations.

As a rule, Indian testimony was discounted because it was in apparent conflict with known facts and theories. Fear of reprisals may account for some of these distortions, while a general misunderstanding of the Indian frame of mind contributed to the problem. In addition to these facts, their statements were subject to unintentional forgetfulness caused by the passage of time, and also the socially accepted practice of embellishment, indulged in at times at the expense of the gullible white man.

Social esteem among the warlike Sioux and Cheyennes was measured by the military achievements of the individual. As a rule, therefore, warfare was waged for the greater glorification of the combatants. Loosely adhering to a common objective, each warrior applied his martial skills as he saw best fit to further his own interest. Other than planning and coordination, Indian leaders had very little control over the conduct of each participant.

The Indian recollections of the Custer Battle are basically personal recountings of incidents which rarely present an overall view. Their statements were based on a series of impressions, conveying only that which had come under the narrator's personal observation. These statements often lacked any reference to time and place. The Indian was interested in his combat performance only and later related his feats during kill-talks, a socially accepted form of bragging about one's accomplishments.

The cultural differences of the Indian are brought to expression in his recollections. It comes as no surprise, therefore, that the Caucasian mind judged these statements as confused, contradictory, and often in contrast with the known reality. Because of these irreconcilable differences, some researchers selected only Indian statements which suited their theories, while others ignored them altogether. Notwithstanding the shortcomings, the Indian side of the story offers a challenging and potentially valuable source of knowledge which, fortunately, has received a measure of creditability through the research of a handful of scholars.

The interviews contained in this volume were recorded by men genuinely interested in the American Indian. One of these was Eli S. Ricker who was a lawyer, a judge, an editor, and a historian. Ricker was born in Maine in 1843, and later moved to Oneida, Illinois, where he enlisted in the Volunteer Infantry during the turbulant Civil War years. He was admitted to the bar in 1885, and then moved to Nebraska where he built a law practice. Ricker became a county judge in 1890, and served as editor of the Chadron *Times* during 1903 and 1904. From 1905 till 1926, he dedicated himself to research for an intended volume about the Indians, which he titled, "The Final Conflict Between the Red Man and the Pale Faces." Ricker became engrossed in his research, and in the process he was able to amass a remarkable collection of source material, including interviews with soldiers, Indians, cowboys, trappers, and generally anyone with knowledge of the frontier and related incidents. Upon his death in 1926, his research collection numbered some 3500 items, among which were more than two hundred notebooks in which he had transcribed his interviews. This volume contains Ricker's interviews with Respects Nothing, Nicholas Ruleau, Flying Hawk, Standing Bear, and Iron Hawk.

The second contributor to this volume is Gen. Hugh L. Scott. Born in Danville, Kentucky, in 1853, Scott attended the West Point Military Academy from 1871 through 1876, when he graduated. The same year he obtained a commission in the Seventh U.S. Cavalry, filling one of the second lieutenant vacancies created by the Custer Fight. Gen. Scott served his country well, rising in rank from lieutenant to brigadier general, from Chief of Staff to Acting

Secretary of War. In his forty-three years of illustrious career, he served in Cuba during the Spanish-American War, in the Phillippines, in West Point as superintendent of the academy, and in England and France during World War I. Scott retired in 1919. He had an abiding interest in the Indian, having mastered their sign language. His large collection of correspondence, memoranda, reports, and papers contain a wealth of information on the subjects of archaeology, ethnography, and sign language. Scott died in 1934. His interviews with He Dog and Red Feather are included in this volume.

One of the more colorful contributors is Judge Frank B. Zahn. Born along the Cannonball River in North Dakota, in 1891, Zahn was the son of William P. Zahn and a Hunkpapa mother. He attended schools at Ft. Yates, Carlisle Indian School, and Riggs Institute. Zahn later served in the armed forces during World War I. He spoke the Teton and Yanktonai Sioux dialects fluently, as well as English and German. Zahn served as an interpreter for twenty-six years, commencing in 1911. He was a freelance writer who wrote a regular feature column for the Ft. Yates newspaper and collaborated with a number of authors in writing books. He served on the Standing Rock Agency tribal council, and eventually became senior judge on the Court of Indian Offenses. Judge Zahn passed away in 1966. His interview with Moving Robe Woman is included in this volume.

The fourth contributor to this volume is Dr. John G. Neihardt. Born in Sharpsburg, Illinois, in 1881, Neihardt graduated from Nebraska Normal College in 1897, and eventually received the distinct honor of becoming Poet Laureate of the State of Nebraska in 1921. From 1946 until 1966 he served on the faculty of the University of Missouri at Columbia. He was internationally known and respected as a historian and authority on the Sioux and Omaha Indians. His greatest accomplishment, however, was his indefatigable writing which produced some twenty-five volumes of poetry, philosophy, and biography. Dr. Neihardt passed away in 1973. This volume contains his interview with Eagle Elk.

The name of Stanley Vestal needs very little introduction. Born as Walter S. Campbell in rural Kansas in 1887, his family eventually moved to Guthrie, Oklahoma Territory, in 1903. He was a Rhodes Scholar, graduating from Oxford in 1911, and accepted a faculty position with the University of Oklahoma in 1915, which institution he served for more than forty years. Campbell enlisted in the armed forces during World War I and served in southern France during the latter part of 1918, and 1919. He was a novelist, a biographer, a historian, a master teacher of writers, and above all, an exhaustive researcher. Campbell published twenty-four books, some 150 journal and magazine articles, and five radio scripts. He died in 1957. Included in this volume is Campbell's interview with White Bull.

The sixth contributor is Walter Mason Camp. Like Ricker, Camp had an enduring interest in the Plains Indians and their wars. Camp was born in Campstown, Pennsylvania, in 1867. In 1883, he entered a career in the railway service which would span a period of some 40 years. Graduating from Pennsylvania State College in 1891, he became an engineer the following year, and was promoted to superintendent of the Rainier Avenue Electric Railway in Seattle, Washington, a few years later. In 1897, he became the editor of the *Railway and Engineering Review*, which position he served until his death in 1925. As did Ricker, Camp devoted the last twenty years of his life to avocational research on the American Indian wars. Known to his Lakota friends by the name of Wicati (Camp), he was described as a quiet, unassuming man who was highly respected for his talents and his knowledge. Camp seemed to have had a tireless pen, an intense interest in the Western Indians, and an indefatigable will to pursue the historical truth. During the course of his research, he established a legacy for himself and those he interviewed, which will forever live in the annals of the American Indian history. By 1925, Camp had completed a chapter outline of his manuscript for his publisher; but his untimely death the same year delayed publication half a century, until 1976, when only a small part of it was made available. Included in this volume are Camp's interviews with Two Eagles, Lone Bear, Lights, Hollow Horn Bear, and Julia Face.

The final contributor is Richard Throssel, a noted Indian artist and photographer who was known among the Crow People in Montana by his native name of Esquon Dupahs. Throssel's interview with the Cheyenne, Two Moons, is included in this volume. These, then, are the distinguised individuals who made this publication possible.

The editing of this compilation was completed through the assistance of the following individuals and institutions. They have earned my enduring gratitude. James Hanson, Director of the Nebraska State Historical Society, for permission to publish the Ricker interviews; James R. Glenn, National Anthropological Archives, Smithsonian, for locating the Scott interviews and the permission to publish the same; and also Kathleen Baxter, of the same institution, for her assistance on numerous occasions; Emmett D. Chisum, Research Historian, University of Wyoming Heritage Center, whose enduring patience with my demanding requests resulted in locating the clippings of the interviews with Moving Robe Woman and Two Moons; Randy Roberts, Senior Manuscript Specialist, University of Missouri Library, whose kind assistance led to the permission by Hilda Neihardt Petri and the John G. Neihardt Trust to publish the extract of the Eagle Elk interview; Brad Koplowitz, Assistant Curator, University of Oklahoma Library, for permission to publish the White Bull interview, and also Brad E. Gernand, of the same institution, who patiently answered my many inquiries; Neil C. Mangum, Chief Historian, Custer Battlefield National Monument, for his gracious assistance and permission to publish the Weston interviews in the Camp Collection; Linda Weirather, Librarian, Parmly Billings Library, for her thoughtfulness in supplying documents; Mari T. Capps, Librarian, West Point Military Academy, for her efforts to locate photographic materials; and finally, the ever gracious Beatrice A. Hight, University of New Mexico Library, who as usual went far beyond my expectation in supplying information.

I am especially indebted to the following two individuals: Wayne Wells, of Smithville, Tennessee, whose scholarly traits led to the discovery of the White Bull manuscript and the Weston interviews, and who then graciously submitted this material to me for my consideration. Secondly, my wife Renée, for her assistance and encouragement, which made it possible for me to complete my research in due time.

RICHARD G. HARDORFF
DeKalb, Illinois
April 5, 1990

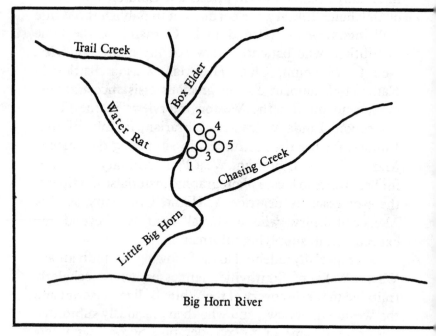

MAP OF RESPECTS NOTHING

1 was the camp of the Cheyennes
2 was the camp of the Uncpapas
3 was the camp of the Itazapcho (Uses Bow)
4 was the camp of the Minneconjous
5 was the camp of the Oglalas[2]

The Respects Nothing Interview

Editorial note: This interview was conducted in 1906 by Eli S. Ricker. The interview resulted in twenty-two pages of text and one map, recorded in longhand on a tablet in Ricker's handwriting. The following is a verbatim transcript of the microfilm copy of the manuscript.

Interview with Respects Nothing who was in the Custer Battle.
Frank Galligo, Interpreter
On White River at mouth of Grass Creek,
November 9, 1906.[1]

Respects Nothing says:
He makes a map on the ground as follows: [see page 24]

He says all these Indians were encamped on a mile square of land, that is to say, on a section. Respects Nothing

---

[1] Respects Nothing was a Northern Oglala Lakota. The correct English translation of his name is Fears Nothing. This interview is contained in the Eli S. Ricker Collection, Nebraska State Historical Society, reel 5, tablet 29, pp. 1-24.

[2] Water Rat Creek, or Muskrat Creek, is the Lakota name for present Medicine Tail Coulee, so named by the Crow Indians who inhabit this region. Respects Nothing has located the Minneconjou camp too far inland. The Minneconjous themselves recall that their camp was situated across from Medicine Tail Ford, which in the early days was significantly known as the Minneconjou Ford. The correct English translation of "Itazapcho" is *not* Uses Bow Band, but rather No Bows Band, which was the name by which the early French identified this subdivision of the Lakotas.

and his wife, White Cow Robe, both tell me that Custer's advance was discovered in this way: Some Oglalas had started for the Red Cloud Agency. One of the number was slow in getting started and was behind. The others had gone forward, and he was following; he saw the dust rising from Custer's column, and also saw the soldiers; he went back and notified the Indians.[3] This was on the morning the battle began.

Reno crossed at the mouth of Trail Creek.[4] When the Indian returned and gave warning of the approach of Custer there was a good deal of excitement and a rush was made for the ponies, and before the people could get out, the village was attacked.

Reno crossed and came down the bottom of the river to the mouth of the Box Elder and began firing from a clump of woods at that point.[5] The Indians left their lodges standing. The women fled down the river, toward the mouth of Chasing Creek.[6] The women did not run back to the hills. Some warriors from all the camps went up to the head of Box Elder Creek and there attacked Reno's line and drove it down into the timber.[7]

Respects Nothing had his horses down below the Indian

---

[3] This may have been the Oglala Lakota, Black Bear. Questioned in 1911 about this matter, Black Bear still seemed afraid to talk about his involvement in events which had taken place some thirty-five years earlier. See Kenneth Hammer, *Custer in '76: Walter Camp's Notes on the Custer Fight* (Provo, 1976), pp. 203-04; J.J. Boesl to Walter Camp, 9/4/1911, Walter Camp Notes, transcript, p. 635, Brigham Young University Library.

[4] Trail Creek is the Lakota identification of the present Reno Creek, named after Major Marcus A. Reno who led Companies A,M, and G of the Seventh Cavalry in an abortive attack on the southern end of the Indian village. For a biography of Reno, see John Upton Terrell and George Walton, *Faint the Trumpet Sounds* (New York, 1966).

[5] Box Elder Creek is the Lakota name for the present Shoulder Blade Creek.

[6] Chasing Creek is probably the Lakota name for present Squaw Creek.

[7] Quick to see a strategical vantage point, Lakotas from all bands collected on the bluffs just south of the mouth of Box Elder Creek (Shoulder Blade Creek). Eventually they charged and pressured Reno's left flank, forcing his command to seek shelter in the dry riverbed along the edge of the woods; see the account of the Lakota, Runs the Enemy, in Joseph K. Dixon, *The Vanishing Race* (New York, 1972), pp. 172-73.

camps and was waiting for his horses to be brought; and when they came he went right up close to the river to the point where Reno was when he had been driven into the timber, and there is where Respects Nothing began to take part. Reno fell back and recrossed the river and ascended the hills where he made his stand. He saw the pack mules come but did not see Benteen's command.[8] There were some soldiers between Reno's main body and the river [who] retreated up the stream to the point of Reno's crossing in retreat and most of them were killed along the river before they could cross.

After Reno was up on the bluffs he was surrounded. Some of the soldiers went down to the river to get water with their hats and the Indians fired on them. They ran back to the position on the hills. Just as Reno reached the hills, Respect Nothing heard an Indian on the north side of the river, and down below a little where Reno had crossed, say that soldiers were coming down behind the ridge.[9]

On the 17th of June they fought under Crazy Horse on the Rosebud and fell back and stayed in the first camp two nights; then fell back in one day to the Little Big Horn and stayed two nights on that river before crossing, and crossed above the mouth of Trail Creek; then they crossed and made camp in the Oglala camp with the other Indians. He says that all these five tribes or bands fell back to the Little Big Horn together, as all of these were in battle together against Crook, June 17th.[10]

[8] Captain Frederick W. Benteen who commanded Companies D, H, and K of the Seventh Cavalry. For an excellent biography of Benteen, see Charles K. Mills, *Harvest of Barren Regrets* (Glendale, 1985).

[9] This was General George A. Custer's battalion, consisting of companies I, L, and C under command of Captain Myles W. Keogh, and Companies E and F commanded by Captain George Yates. Apparently, Custer's battalion was then descending Cedar Coulee. For evidence relating to these assignments, see Richard G. Hardorff, *Markers, Artifacts and Indian Testimony* (Short Hills, 1985), p. 24.

He says the Indians had no expectation that the soldiers would follow. After the fight with Crook, some of the Indian scouts went back to see what Crook's soldiers were doing, and they found that Crook was falling back, and so they did not expect any further fighting.

(He saw Custer's horse which was a chestnut sorrel with stocking legs.[11] He saw Custer's clothing which was buckskin, after Custer was killed.)

(Eagle Ring was eleven (11) years old at the time of the battle and went on the field with the old women. They stripped the dead naked and the women struck the bodies with sticks as in coups, but did not mutilate the bodies. Eagle Ring was present at this interview with Respects Nothing.)

Next day after the Custer battle an Indian went up on the high hill where I went up and with a field glass (probably taken from the dead on the Custer field) looked down the river and saw Terry's soldiers late in the afternoon.[12] They quit Reno and went down and confronted Terry and had a little fight there and took some horses from Terry; then they fell back to their old camp and took their lodges with them, leaving only one lodge in which they left their dead.[13] They left 20 dead on the battlefield—20 dead on the battlefield

---

[10]Reference is made to the battle of the Rosebud, June 17, 1876, when a united force of Sioux and Cheyennes fought a victory over units of the Second and Third Cavalry and Fourth and Ninth Infantry, the whole commanded by General George Crook. In view of the length of this battle and the ammunition expended, it seems almost incredible that the casualty count amounted to only nine troopers and about six Indians. One of the best studies of this battle is J.W. Vaughn, *With Crook at the Rosebud* (Harrisburg, 1956).

[11]On June 25, 1876, Custer rode Vic, abbreviated from *victory,* a sorrel horse with four white feet and a blaze in his face; see John Burkman, Custer's orderly, to Elizabeth Custer, 2/3/1911, Elizabeth B. Custer Collection, roll 3, Custer Battlefield National Monument; William A. Graham, *The Custer Myth* (New York, 1953), p. 345.

[12]General Alfred H. Terry who commanded the Department of Dakota and who accompanied the Montana Column.

[13]Military eyewitnesses discovered two lodges standing on the benchland opposite the

[*sic*], and two others died on Wood Lice Creek. These were all they lost altogether.[14]

They fell back before Terry to Box Elder and stopped there a little while, then continued to retreat up the river to the mouth of the Wood Lice Creek about 15 miles, where they arrived at daylight next morning. They stayed here two days and then went up to the head of Wood Lice Creek in the mountains; stayed there two days and went across, going east, to the head of the Little Big Horn River, and were there about two days; from here they moved over to Tongue River; they went back from the head of the Little Big Horn to the Rosebud; when they were camped on the head of the Little Big Horn they killed a Cheyenne scout, and attacked a party of soldiers in which was Baptiste Pourier and Frank Grouard, and got their horses (This must have been the Sibley scout.)[15]

From the Rosebud station they went right down the river, camping two or three times; then they moved to Tongue River and followed down that river, thence over to the Powder River, thence went to the Cottonwood River, thence to Beaver Creek; then the next camp was on Tinder Creek, then moved to Picket Pin Butte, then to the Grand River, on the head of this Frank Grouard captured some

mouth of present Deep Ravine. One lodge revealed the remains of five warriors, while the other contained only three; Usher L. Burdick, *Tales from the Buffalo Land* (Baltimore, 1940), p. 52; Col. John Gibbon, "Last Summer's Expedition Against the Sioux," *American Catholic Quarterly Review* (April, 1877): 297.

[14]Respects Nothing's total of twenty killed has reference to the body count of slain Lakotas only. On Wood Louse Creek, known to the Crow Indians as Little Fat Creek, the Minneconjou, Three Bears, and the Oglala, Black White Man, died from the trauma of their wounds; see Raymond J. DeMallie, *The Sixth Grandfather* (Lincoln, 1984), pp. 196, 198. For a listing of Indian casualties, see the White Bull interview hereafter.

[15]On July 7, 1876, Lt. Frederick W. Sibley, Second Cavalry, and a detachment of twenty-five troopers and four civilians encountered a force of Cheyennes near the headwaters of the Little Bighorn who nearly succeeded in capturing the entire command. After a short fight, Sibley abandoned his horses and escaped on foot. The only casualty

Indians and the Indians took some horses from the soldiers.[16] From the head of Grand River the Oglalas and Cheyennes separated from the others and turned towards the Black Hills and camped on Box Elder. The three other tribes went down to the mouth of the Yellowstone and crossed the Missouri there.

The Oglalas and Cheyennes moved next to Pole Creek; at this place the two tribes split and the former went to Tongue River, and the Cheyennes followed Pole Creek up to the Powder River. The Oglalas then went to the head of the Rosebud, then down the Rosebud and camped on the Cheyenne Creek; they stayed around in that country the rest of the season and did some fighting with the Crows but no more with the soldiers.

---

was a Cheyenne named Tall Bear, better known by his Sioux name White Antelope. For an eyewitness account, see John F. Finerty, *War-path and Bivouac* (Norman, 1961). Of French descent, Baptiste Pourier, better known as Big Bat, was born in St. Charles, Missouri, on July 18, 1842. At age fourteen, he found employment as a teamster and moved with Indian traders into the country west of the Mississippi. In this capacity, he gained a thorough knowledge of the country and the Sioux language. Eventually, he married Josephine Richard, an Oglala mixed-blood of French extraction. Pourier's expertise was recognized by the military authorities who employed him as a scout, guide, and interpreter from 1869 on. He passed away in 1932. See the James McLaughlin letter, dated 8/30/1920, in the South Dakota State Historical Society, to which is appended Pourier's affidavit, filed on his behalf by McLaughlin to seek a government pension. Born on September 20, 1853, Frank Grouard was captured by Sioux Indians in 1869, and remained among them for the next five years. For a biography of this individual, see Joe DeBarthe, *Life and Adventures of Frank Grouard* (Norman, 1958). Frank Grouard passed away on August 20, 1905, at St. Joseph Missouri, where he was interred in the Ashland Cemetery. History has not been kind to Grouard, and scholars are still debating whether he was a mixed-blood Lakota or a Mulatto who lied about his ancestry. Grouard himself consistently repeated that he was born in Tahiti, on the Isle of Taiarapu. Newly discovered evidence corroborates his claim; see Richard G. Hardorff, "The Frank Grouard Geneology," *Custer and His Times, Book Two* (Fort Worth, 1984), pp. 123-33.

[16] On September 10, 1876, Captain Anson Mills and two battalions of the Third Cavalry captured a Minneconjou village of thirty-six lodges near Slim Buttes, present South Dakota. The casualty total consisted of one trooper, one civilian, and six Lakotas, among which was the Minneconjou leader Iron Shield. For an excellent study of this engagement, see Jerome A. Greene, *Slim Buttes, 1876: An Episode of the Great Sioux War* (Norman, 1982).

Custer came down on top of the ridge northeast of Water Rat Creek. He did not come to the river, or directly attempt to [do so]. He came over from that ridge [and moved] to Calhoun Hill where the battle began.[17] The stones in the cemetery at the southeast, or rather in the line running down toward the river from Calhoun Hill, is where the battle began, and it is plain to be seen that an effort was made at that point to check the advance of the Indians, and a good many soldiers fell here.[18] It should be said that the Indians attacking at this point had crossed the Little Big Horn at the mouth of Water Rat (or what Godfrey names in his map as Reno Creek).[19]

The soldiers came up to Calhoun Hill diagonally from the east, and the Indians came up diagonally from the river crossing to Calhoun Hill. These Indians enveloped the ridge on the north side about half way and were met by Indians who had crossed the river at the lower crossing, just below the corner of the cemetery, and [who] enveloped the

---

[17]The "ridge northeast of Water Rat" (see map) is most likely the present Luce Ridge, which is situated along the north bank of Medicine Tail Coulee. This ridge curves at its eastern end into Nye-Cartwright Ridge, about a mile east of the river, which spur then runs westward to Calhoun Hill. Luce Ridge was named after Captain Edward S. Luce, Custer Battlefield superintendent from 1940 through 1956, who discovered a concentration of military artifacts at this location. Nye-Cartwright Ridge was named after Ralph G. Cartwright, a schoolteacher in Lead, South Dakota, and Lt. Col. Edward L. Nye whose interest in the Custer Battle led to the discovery of hundreds of casings on the latter ridge.

[18]Reference is made to the western terminus of Calhoun Hill, known to the Lakotas as Greasy Grass Hill, which location contained the bodies of some twenty slain troopers and two non-commissioned officers, the latter of C Company. Numerous military and Indian artifacts have been found along and near this ridge; see Jerome A. Greene, *Evidence and the Custer Enigma* (Reno, 1979), p. 28 and the accompanying map. Calhoun Hill was named after Lt. James Calhoun, L Company, Seventh Cavalry, who was slain with his men at this location.

[19]General Edward S. Godfrey. Ranked a lieutenant in 1876, he commanded K Company in Benteen's battalion. The map spoken of appeared in Godfrey's article, "Custer's Last Battle," which was published in the *Century Magazine* of January, 1892. Before the turn of the century, Medicine Tail Coulee was known as Reno Creek.

ridge on the north side of the ridge after coming up the nose of the ridge to the northwest. Some Indians crossed the river above this lower crossing, probably at the mouth of the ravine. The soldiers were completely surrounded.[20]

The battle began about one o'clock p.m. and lasted till four o'clock p.m. The man who came back and gave notice that the soldiers were coming had a watch which was taken from someone of Crook's dead soldiers in the battle of the 17th of June on the Rosebud, and this watch showed the time to the Indians. Moreover, to test Respects Nothing, I took him outside the house and asked him to point where the sun stood when the battle was commenced by Reno, and he correctly indicated the quarter of the heavens where it would be at that time.

Custer's line was along the ridge, but it is not clear to my mind from his statement whether Custer stopped to fight before he reached his last place; but I think that he said Custer went to that point finally and the last defenders were killed here. At any rate, he said that those were all killed at Custer Hill before those were down along the ravine. These latter, when the others were down, made a break through a narrow gap in the Indian line and ran toward the river trying to escape. They were on foot. The Indians followed them and killed them with war clubs of stone and wooden clubs, some of the latter having lance spears on them. In this pursuit one Indian stumbled into a low place, among the soldiers, and was killed by them.[21]

---

[20] Just below (downstream) the northwest corner of the present boundary fence lies a river crossing which leads to a natural passageway around and to the northeast of Custer Hill. Upstream from this lower crossing was yet another ford, sometimes called Cheyenne Ford, which lies directly opposite the mouth of Deep Ravine, the latter not to be confused with Deep Coulee which runs along the southside of Calhoun Hill.

[21] The "low place" is the present Deep Ravine in which the bodies of 28 of Custer's men were discovered by military survivors two days after the battle. Respects Nothing makes clear that the battle ended with the killing of these men. The Indian killed at this location

Respects Nothing says that the fighting with Reno was all over before Custer was engaged. Respects Nothing says that he helped drive Reno across the river, and then he galloped down to the crossing at the mouth of Water Rat, or Reno Creek, and crossed and went up and fought on the north side of the ridge and at Custer Hill. One Indian dashed right through the soldiers at Custer Hill on horseback. I have forgotten whether he said this Indian was killed, but I think he said he was killed.[22]

One soldier attempted to get away on horseback from Calhoun Hill and was a long way off when he was killed by pursuing Indians.[23]

Reno could have gone to the aid of Custer if he had moved when the Indians withdrew. They went down and attacked Custer. Why should not Reno have gone down and helped in the defense? The Indians were all fighting Reno in the first battle.

Respects Nothing says the Indians took 700 guns as spoils. This must be an error.[24] Respects Nothing is an able Indian. He made a clear map on the ground floor of Frank

was the Cheyenne, Noisy Walking, known to the Lakotas as Left Hand. He was the son of the prominent Cheyenne, White Bull, whose nickname was Ice; see Thomas B. Marquis, *Wooden Leg* (Lincoln, 1962), p. 241.

[22]This act of valor was performed by Bearded Man, a Southern Cheyenne chief of the Elk Society, known to his own people as Lame White Man. He was killed just south of Custer Hill and, being mistaken for a Ree Indian Scout, he was scalped and otherwise mutilated by the Minneconjou Lakota, Little Crow; see Stanley Vestal, *Warpath* (Boston, 1934), p. 199; De Mallie, *The Sixth Grandfather* p. 186. The alleged location where Lame White Man was slain was marked under the direction of his grandson, John Stands in Timber, by a wooden cross placed by the National Park Service on the river side of the blacktop on Custer Ridge, John Stands in Timber aned Margot Liberty, *Cheyenne Memories* (Lincoln, 1972), p. 203, n23.

[23]Nearly every Indian eyewitness makes reference to this or other attempted escapes, the end result being inevitably the same in that the soldier either suicided or was shot in the back; see, for instance, the pictographs by Amos Bad Heart Bull in Helen H. Blish, *A Pictographic History of the Oglala Sioux* (Lincoln, 1967), pp. 269-72; George B. Grinnell *The Fighting Cheyennes* (Norman, 1956), p. 353; Stands in Timber and Liberty, *Cheyenne Memories*, pp. 207-08.

Galligo's new house, and by the aid of it gave a concise and clear description of all the events of the fighting. I think no white man could have given a better account. He confirmed exactly all those things which are known of these battles; and this fact is evidential that what he stated that is not known to the world, is true. He said he would tell me nothing but the facts as he knew them, and I am sure he did. He is an intelligent man.

[24] Inasmuch as the total casualties of both Custer's and Reno's battles amounted to some 260 men, the maximum stand of revolvers, carbines, and rifles could not have been much more than 520 pieces. Yet, some Indian accounts are persistent in their tally of 700; see Blish, *Pictographic History*, p. 272; M.I. McCreight, *Firewater and Forked Tongues* (Pasadena, 1947), p. 114.

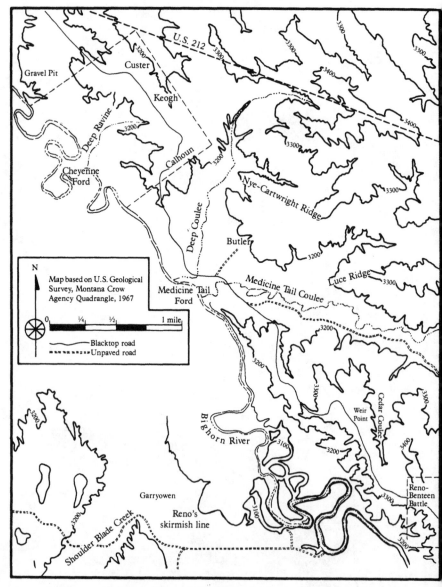

Editor's Map of the Little Bighorn Battlefield

The Nicholas Ruleau Interview

Editorial note: This interview was conducted in 1906 by Eli S. Ricker. The interview resulted in sixteen pages of text and one map, recorded in longhand on a tablet in Ricker's handwriting. The following is a verbatim transcript of the microfilm copy of the manuscript.

Interview with Nicholas Ruleau.
At Pine Ridge,
Nov. 20, 1906.[1]

He has lived on this Reservation since 1879, and he has acted as interpreter for a good many who talked with Indians who were in the Custer battle, and in this way has obtained a good knowledge concerning that disaster. He says:

Minneconjous means "Plants along the water." Sitting Bull's band was the Uncpapa.

He brings me a map prepared by Austin Red Hawk for him; also the names of the bands of Indians who were camped on the Little Big Horn, as follows:

---

[1] Nick Ruleau was of French extraction. He was engaged in the fur trade during its waning days. This interview is contained in the Eli S. Ricker Collection, Nebraska State Historical Society, reel 5, tablet 29, pp. 84-99.

Oglala Sioux, Crazy Horse, chief, 350 warriors or braves
Uncpapas, Sitting Bull, chief, 1000 warriors
Minneconjous, Buffalo Bull, chief, 700 warriors[2]
Uses Bow, Spotted Eagle, chief, 300 warriors
Cheyennes, Little Coyote, 45 warriors[3]
Rosebuds (Brule Sioux), Flying Chaser, chief, 80 warriors
Santees, Red Top, chief, 40 warriors
Yanktons, White Eagle, chief, abt. 40 warriors

There were about 6000 men, women and children in the camps. Mr. Nick Ruleau says many of these warriors—probably one-third—were single men, [which] is the reason why there were not more people in the camp as compared with the number of braves.[4]

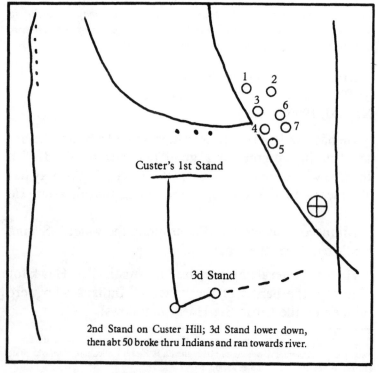

MAP OF NICHOLAS RULEAU

Explanation of the map:

1 Uncpapas	5 Cheyennes	⊕ This is the point to
2 Oglalas	6 Yankton	which the camps—old
3 Minneconjous	7 Santees	men, women, and
4 Uses Bows		children—fled and
		collected[5]

Mr. Nick Ruleau says he has this account from Austin Red Hawk and Shot in the Face, Big Road (dead) and Iron Bull. These all agreed in statements.[6] He has talked with others who had been wounded but did not see the battle through.

Red Hawk says about three hundred (300) were killed in the battle and two hundred (200) died in the camps from wounds as they were moving over the country.[7]

These men said that Reno began his action about nine

---

[2]Buffalo Bull was a minor war chief. The patriarch councilor of the Minneconjou Lakotas was Lone Horn who died of old age in his lodge on the Cheyenne River in 1875, whereupon his four sons became leaders of small kinship units. Their names were Big Foot, also known as Spotted Elk (1826-1890), Roman Nose, Frog, and Touch the Clouds (1836-1905); see Richard G. Hardorff, *The Oglala Lakota Crazy Horse* (Mattituck, 1985), p. 27. The Minneconjou band chiefs present at the Little Bighorn were Makes Room, Lame Deer, Black Shield, and Touch the Clouds; see Walter M. Camp Manuscripts, Indiana University Library, p. 348.

[3]The estimate of 45 Cheyenne warriors appears to be much too low. The Cheyenne, Wooden Leg, estimated the number of his people at the Little Bighorn at 1600, while his kinsmen Tall Bull and White Bull told Walter Camp that their encampment consisted of 200 lodges and 3000 people. See Marquis, *Wooden Leg*, p. 206; Hammer, *Custer in '76*, pp. 211-12. For an enlightening view on this subject, see the study by Harry H. Anderson, "Cheyennes at the Little Big Horn: A Study of Statistics," *North Dakota History* (Spring, 1960): 81-93. Anderson arrived at the conclusion that the Cheyennes numbered only 70 lodges, containing 90 warriors and 500 people in all.

[4]Ruleau's population figure of 6000 is about half the estimated total of most witnesses. However, when compared with recent studies, his total appears to be in line. See John S. Gray's monograph in the *Centennial Campaign: The Sioux War of 1876* (Fort Collins, 1976), p. 357. Dr. Gray deduced the total Indian population at the Little Bighorn at 1000 lodges, containing 7120 persons, including 1780 adult males; and also Robert A. Marshall, "How Many Indians Were There?" *The Research Review* (June, 1977):8, who estimated a ceiling of 795 lodges and a corresponding population of 5056 people.

[5]The location of the Oglala circle seems to be incorrect. The Oglalas, and most other Lakotas, indicate that their camp was on the flat just southwest of the Cheyenne encampment.

o'clock in the morning.[8] The Indians mounted their horses and went to where the soldiers were and found them lined up at the head of Muddy Creek.[9] The Indians waited till enough of them got together. Crazy Horse said to his followers: "Here are some of the soldiers after us again. Do your best, and let us kill them all off today, that they may not trouble us anymore. All ready! Charge!" himself leading the assault.[10] The soldiers tried hard to hold their

[6] Big Road, more accurately translated as Wide Road, was a chief of a Bad Face band of Northern Oglalas. He was an intelligent, but unreconstructed man who preferred exile in Canada in 1877 rather than reservation life on one of the Missouri agencies. For an account of his stay in Canada with Sitting Bull, see Stanley Huntley's interview with the hostile Sioux in the *Chicago Daily Tribune* of July 5, 1879. The other three Lakotas have not been positively identified.

[7] In view of the casualty totals obtained from other eyewitnesses, Ruleau's hearsay numbers are too exaggerated to merit serious consideration. See the casualty count in the White Bull interview.

[8] At the Inquiry in 1879, Lt. George Wallace, the official itinerist, made clear that his watch readings did *not* represent *local sun time,* but rather Chicago time, which was the official time maintained at Fort Abraham Lincoln. Lt. Edward S. Godfrey made clear that the watches of the officers had not been changed since leaving Fort Lincoln. Thus, as a result of the watch readings submitted by Lt. Wallace, scholars have come to a general agreement that Reno's valley battle commenced about 3 p.m., Chicago time. However, it should be noted that the difference between Chicago time and the far west (San Francisco time) was then calculated to be some 2¼ hours, which follows that the valley fight started at about 1 o'clock far western time. Since the watch recovered at the Rosebud battlefield may have carried San Francisco time, it does not seem impossible that it was still operative a week later when, according to Respects Nothing, it was read by one of the (agency or mixed blood) Indians. See William A. Graham, *Abstract of the Official Record of the Reno Court of Inquiry* (Harrisburg, 1954), p. 37.

[9] Muddy Creek is probably yet another name for Shoulder Blade Creek. In my estimation, it probably refers to the mouth of this creek which sheltered many of the Indians early in Reno's valley fight. See J. W. Vaughn, *Indian Fights* (Norman, 1966), pp. 145-166, which gives a survey of Shoulderblade, its drainage area, and the positions of Reno's skirmish lines.

[10] Crazy Horse was an Oglala Lakota who was born near Bear Butte, South Dakota, in 1840. He was one of the most respected individuals among the warlike Sioux, and his name became the epitome of Indian resistance to white encroachment. While resisting arrest, he was bayonetted by Pvt. William Gentles at Camp Robinson, Nebraska, on September 5, 1877. He passed away the same day. For a stirring biography of this individual, see Mari Sandoz, *Crazy Horse: The Strange Man of the Oglalas* (Lincoln, 1961); Richard G. Hardorff, *The Oglala Lakota Crazy Horse: A Preliminary Genealogical Study and An Annotated Listing of Primary Sources* (Mattituck, 1985).

ground but were outnumbered; so they took their horses and retreated. The Indians chased the soldiers across the river, killing about 40. They chased them up on the bluff or high point where the [pack] train was, and had the soldiers coralled in a small place.[11]

While they had the soldiers at this point fighting, one of the Indians gave notice that there were soldiers coming at the other end. So most of the Indians left Reno and went to fight the other soldiers. These latter soldiers were coming down on the ridge in three divisions. They did not come down to the river. The first division came to a point about half a mile or three quarters of a mile from the river.[12] The Indians fell back down the river bottom through the village

---

[11] The pack train and its escort did not arrive until an hour after Reno had gained the bluffs. Ruleau is correct as to his number of 40 slain of Reno's command, which breaks down as follows: 3 officers, 32 enlisted men, 3 Ree Indian Scouts, and 2 civilians; see John S. Gray's monograph in the *Centennial Campaign*, pp. 291-95.

[12] One of the most debated issues of the Custer Battle centers around the question whether Custer attempted to cross the river. Was an attempt made to cross at Medicine Tail Ford *before* his command was forced back toward Calhoun Hill? Or was it never near the ford, but instead did his command travel straight from Cedar Coulee to Calhoun Hill? The early Cheyenne statements suggest that Custer indeed reached the river and had quite a spirited engagement there. However, the later Cheyenne accounts refute any combat at the crossing. Instead, these sources assert that Custer went directly to Calhoun Hill, and that his closest position to the stream was held by troopers at that location. The same bewildering contradiction holds true for the Sioux accounts, which are equally divided on this issue. However, modern field research now has established that soldiers were deployed near the ford and also on Luce Ridge, the heights situated along the north bank of Medicine Tail Coulee, about one mile east of the river. A reconstruction of the combat scenario suggests that the troops near the crossing were withdrawn to Calhoun Hill before those on Luce Ridge followed. This latter movement was observed by the recent Indian reinforcements coming from the Reno fight, which might explain why these warriors categorically denied any combat action at the ford. Of course, we have to be careful with our conception of "at" and "near" which does not necessarily have to mean *at the river's edge*. Ruleau's statement, although hearsay and perhaps subjected to personal impressions, offers us the first indication of three divisions prior to Custer's movement to Calhoun Hill. His further statement that Custer came within a half mile of the river, corroborates the growing evidence that troopers were deployed simultaneously on the flat near the river and also on Luce Ridge. For a listing of artifacts, see Jerome A. Green, *Evidence and the Custer Engima*, pp. 16-18; Hardorff, *Markers, Artifacts, and Indian Testimony*, pp. 24-28.

and crossed the Little Big Horn at the only crossing and went up the high hill in the direction of Reno and from there assailed the leading division.[13]

Crazy Horse and Gall and Knife Chief were haranguing the Indians to get together so they could make another charge on the soldiers. He (Red Hawk) says when the Indians all got together they went down from this point, or hill and met the first division of these soldiers and they fought this back to the second division; from that they

[13] The high hill referred to can only be the cluster of three knobs now known as Weir Point, from which elevation Captain Thomas B. Weir of Benteen's command in vain scanned Custer's battlefield more than an hour later.

[14] This statement, associated with the three dots on the map, seems to suggest that the troops nearest the river were forced eastward onto a second unit, the whole then withdrawing to the balance of Custer's command. A similar observation was made by Curly, a surviving Crow Indian Scout with Custer's battalion, who stated that Custer came down a coulee to its mouth; that the column was "stretched up this deep coulee and away back on side of ridge;" that the Indians' fire then forced the head of the column to retreat to a ridge northeast, where they reunited with the main command. Lt. Charles F. Roe, "The Custer Massacre: Narrative of Curley, a Crow Scout," *The Army and Navy Journal* (March 25, 1882):761.

Gall, also known as Man Who Goes in the Middle, was born in a Hunkpapa Lakota camp on the banks of the Grand River, South Dakota, in 1840. Throughout his non-reservation life he proved himself a fierce opponent to the white aggressors. In November, 1867, the military issued orders for his arrest, and while resisting capture near abandoned Fort Berthold, he was bayonetted entirely through the body from both front and rear and was left for dead. Miraculously, he recovered enough from the shock of his wounds to make his escape before daylight, walking twenty miles in severe winter weather to the house of a relative. Gall survived this ordeal, and it was said that out of vengeance he killed and scalped seven whites, among whom was Lt. Eben Crosby on October 14, 1871. During Reno's attack on the Hunkpapa lodges, Gall's two wives and three children were killed. To avenge his family, he mutilated a number of Custer's soldiers, and fearing reprisals, he took his band to Canada. He surrendered to the U.S. Military at Poplar Creek, Montana, in the winter of 1880. His conduct on the reservation was exemplary, and he later became a justice of the Indian Police Court at Standing Rock Agency. Gall passed away on December 5, 1893 from an overdose of weight-reduction medication. He lies buried at Wakpala, South Dakota. See Lewis F. Crawford, *Rekindling Camp Fires: The Exploits of Ben Arnold* (Bismarck, 1926), pp. 166-68; Usher L. Burdick, *David F. Barry's Indian Notes on the Custer Battle* (Baltimore, 1949), pp. 33, 35; *St. Paul Pioneer Press,* July 18, 1886

Very little information is available on Knife Chief. Apparently, he was a prominent Oglala Lakota and a ranked member of a soldier lodge. During the Ghost dance troubles of the 1890s, he was an active militant, commanding a band of 150 dancers.

drove the two divisions back to the first [third?] division.[14] All this time the soldiers fought bravely; he adds that he never saw soldiers fight like they did. He says several Indians were killed now, but no soldiers were killed. The officers tried their utmost to keep the soldiers together at this point, but the horses were unmanageable; they would rear up and fall backward with their riders; some would get away. The Indians forced the troopers back to where the first stand was made on Calhoun Hill and the ridge running therefrom towards the river.[15] At this place the soldiers stood in line and made a very good fight. The soldiers delivered volley after volley into the dense ranks of the Indians without any perceptible effect on account of their great numbers.[16]

---

[15] Many years after the battle, the location just north of Luce Ridge yielded the remains of four troopers and three horses. These casualties may have occurred during Custer's march to Calhoun Hill, or, more likely, these may have been individuals attempting to escape from Calhoun Hill toward Reno's command. See Greene, *Evidence and the Custer Enigma*, p. 52, items 20-22; and also Marquis, *Wooden Leg*, p. 232, which mentions the escape of four troopers, three of which were killed while a fourth suicided.

[16] These volleys were heard by many of Reno's command then idling on the bluffs some three miles to the south. Initially, some of these volleys were fired from Nye-Cartwright Ridge, where many years later little piles of casings were discovered lying in groups of three. Cheyenne statements reveal that volleys were also fired from Calhoun Ridge, and a survey of this area immediately after the battle disclosed that the soldiers deployed here had offered determined resistance. Officers attested later to having seen piles of casings in the intervals between the slain bodies, some piles containing as many as thiry shells. The fierce struggle for this pivotal location may well have caused eleven of the seventeen alleged Indian casualties on Custer's battlefield; see Hammer, *Custer in '76*, p. 213, which contains Tall Bull's statement about volley firing; Gall's recollection of the number of Indian casualties is contained in the *St. Paul Pioneer Press* of July 18, 1886; while Graham, *Abstract of the Reno Court of Inquiry* contains a wealth of information on the volume of Custer's firing. However, those scholars who profess bewilderment by the apparent contradictions in the Indian accounts of the battle—those who question the veracity of these Indian statements and then dismiss them altogether as being irreconcilable—ought to attempt to explain the contradictions in the officers' testimony given only three years after the battle. Of these seemingly intelligent men, Lt. Charles A. Varnum heard heavy firing, a sort of crash-crash, and he exclaimed, "Jesus Christ, Wallace, hear that—and that[!]" (p. 55); yet, Lt. George Wallace testified he heard no volleys, but only a few scattering shots from the west side of the river (p. 21), while at the same time Lt. Winfield S. Edgerly remembered hearing very heavy volley firing coming

The Indians kept coming like an increasing flood which could not be checked. The soldiers were swept off their feet; they could not stay; the Indians were overwhelming. Here the troopers divided and retreated on each side of the ridge, falling back steadily to Custer Hill where another stand was made.[17] By this time the Indians were taking the guns and cartridges of the dead soldiers and putting these to use and were more active in the struggle. Here the soldiers made a desperate fight. What was left of them retreated to the (what he calls) third stand. These were

---

from downstream (p. 160); but Captain Frederick W. Benteen heard only 15 or 20 shots (p. 139), while Major Marcus A. Reno did not hear any firing and therefore assumed Custer was not engaged at all, Reno blaming his misjudgement on the other officers for failing to inform him of the true situation (p. 227); yet, the veracity of this self-serving statement is in serious doubt, because Captain Thomas M. McDougall heard two dull-sounding volleys and distinctly recalled reporting this to Reno, who became agitated and totally ignored it (pp. 194, 195); however, McDougall's concern was not ignored by Captain Myles Moylan who had heard faint volley firing and who checked with McDougall to confirm it (p. 75); moreover, Lt. Edward S. Godfrey heard two distinct volleys in spite of his natural hearing impairment (p. 178), and he turned to Lt. Luther R. Hare who affirmed it (p. 96). Of the two non-commissioned officers who testified, Sgt. Edward Davern stated he heard indistinctive volley firing while in the presence of Major Reno as his orderly (p. 119), while Sgt. Ferdinand A. Culbertson recalled a couple of very heavy volleys at a time when Reno was near him (p. 125). Of the individuals left behind in the valley upon Reno's retreat, Interpreter Frederick F. Gerard vividly recalled hearing three or four volleys, as if 50 to 100 guns were discharged at a volley (p. 41), while Scout George Herendeen testified he heard a great many volleys and scattering shots, the whole lasting about one hour (p 84); and lastly, Lt. Charles A. DeRudio positively remembered hearing an immense volley firing, which volleys were steady for a long time, and that the whole lasted about an hour and a half before it died out in scattering shots (pp. 107, 110, 111). This, then, is the intelligent testimony of mostly trained military observers, of which the two highest ranking officers conveniently disclaimed hearing any of Custer's volleys at all, while the commanding officer, Major Reno, had the impudence to complain he was not being posted on a matter which progress was being monitored *in his presence*.

[17]It is not quite certain which ridge is meant in the narration. Surviving troopers stationed at the west end of Calhoun Ridge may have withdrawn north and upon crossing Custer Ridge, they may have united with the balance of the regiment then retreating along its eastern slope. See also Graham, *The Custer Myth*, p. 115, which contains a statement by several former hostiles in reference to Calhoun's troop; that this troop made a considerable fight and that nearly all the Indians killed (on Custer's battlefield) fell at this fight; and that this troop soon was driven back to the position where it was overwhelmed with the balance of the command.

surrounded and the Indians rushed on the soldiers. Some of the soldiers broke through the Indians and ran for the ravine, but were all killed without getting into it.[18]

From where they made the third stand a soldier broke away from the Indians and got away. When quite a distance from the Indians—and the Indians had given up the chase—they saw him fall from his horse. They went over to him and found that he had a bullet wound in his right temple. The Indians don't know whether he shot himself or was shot by someone, but they believe he shot himself as they saw nobody near him.[19]

It was about noon when they annihilated Custer and his men.[20] After the battle was over, the Indians stripped the dead bodies of clothing and took their guns and ammunition. The Indians did not scalp any of *Custer's* men; but they did scalp all of Reno's men who were killed. Reno had some Indian scouts with him, some of whom were wounded and were alive; the Indians said these Indians wanted to die—that was what they were scouting with the soldiers for; so they killed them and scalped them.[21]

[18] The second stand, perhaps better known as Keogh's Stand, was a desperate fight which took place on the east slope of Custer Ridge and which involved I Company and survivors from companies C and L. The third stand was on Custer Hill, from which location some forty men fled down the ravine toward the river. Ruleau is in error stating these men were slain along the edge of the ravine because some 28 bodies were found on the bottom of the washout. This statement is a good indication of Ruleau's mental editing, he having gained this impression after viewing the faulty marker locations of these men. For evidence of the true location of these bodies, see Robert M. Utley, *The Reno Court of Inquiry: The Chicago Times Account* (Fort Collins, 1972), pp. 224, 274, containing the testimony by Lts. Hare and DeRudio; and also Hammer, *Custer in '76*, p. 72, McDougall's observations.

[19] This is yet another trooper who attempted to escape. This individual is not to be confused with the soldier observed by Fears Nothing who made the attempted escape from Calhoun Hill.

[20] Of interest here is not the absolute time itself, but rather the opportunity it affords us to figure the length of time expired since the opening of the valley fight, which Ruleau was told started at 9 o'clock in the morning. Converting this into Chicago time (military time), we learn that Reno's battle commenced at 3 p.m., and that Custer's battle ended at 6 p.m.

After the annihilation of Custer's men, the Indians all went back to Reno and besieged him all afternoon, and all night, and all the next day till sundown. Red Hawk says the women did not take any hand in the battle and did not mutilate any of the dead.[22]

About sundown the next day they saw some soldiers coming up the river; so the Indians stopped fighting Reno and moved away that night.[23] If they had fought Reno another day or two, they would have wiped his command out. If the Indians did not kill Reno's men, they would all have died of thirst. Reno made a desperate fight. He managed to keep the Indians from rushing his position.[24]

About a month after the battle some thirty Indians, including Red Hawk, went back to the battlefield and were looking over it. At the mouth of the ravine they found eight

---

[21] Those slain on Custer Hill were farthest away from the village and seemed to have been spared the scalping and extreme disfiguration observed on the field nearer the village. The names of the three slain Rees were Bloody Knife, Bobtail Bull, and Little Soldier. Particular vengeance was directed toward Bloody Knife who was part Hunkpapa Lakota, his body having been decapitated and the head placed on a pole and carried in triumph around the village. Positive identification of the remains of Bobtail Bull and Little Soldier was made impossible due to the obliteration of the facial features by the Sioux. The Ree, Bobtail Bull, was a brother of the Cheyenne, Plenty Crows, the latter having been taken captive by the Cheyennes and raised since a young boy; see Orin G. Libby, *The Arikara Narrative of the Campaign Against the Hostile Dakotas, June 1876* (New York, 1973), pp. 110, 114, 145; Grinnell, *The Fighting Cheyennes*, p. 355; and Stands in Timber and Liberty, *Cheyenne Memories*, p. 209.

[22] Sioux and Cheyennes reported the presence of several women who participated in the assault on Custer's force. One of these was the Hunkpapa, Moving Robe Woman, who avenged the death of her younger brother by slaying several of Custer's troopers; see Charles A. Eastman, "Rain-in-the-Face," *The Outlook* (October 27, 1906):511; and also Floyd S. Maine, *Lone Eagle . . . The White Sioux* (Albuquerque, 1956), pp. 128-29, which recounts the exploits of Walks with Stars Woman, the wife of the Oglala, Crow Dog.

[23] This was General Alfred H. Terry's force of units from the Second Cavalry and Seventh Infantry. The Indian withdrawal was made over the benchland south of Shoulder Blade toward the Big Horn Mountain, late in the afternoon of June 26. Marquis, *Wooden Leg*, p. 270; DeMallie, *The Sixth Grandfather*, p. 296. For an excellent account of Terry's march, see Edward J. McClernand, *With the Indian and the Buffalo in Montana, 1870-1878* (Glendale, 1969). The volume contains McClernand's narrative account and his journal of marches while a lieutenant in G Company, Second Cavalry.

(8) dead soldiers lying with their uniforms on and their guns and ammunition and everything by them. Red Hawk said they could not understand how these soldiers were killed down there.[25] They did not, out of respect for their superstition that if they take anything from any person that has been dead a long time that his spirit will haunt them, remove any of the things which belonged to the 8 dead soldiers.

Sitting Bull took no part in the battle. Gall, Crazy Horse and Knife Chief were the leading chiefs in command. Knife Chief and Crazy Horse were Oglalas. Gall was an Uncpapa. Red Hawk says Rain-in-the-Face was not in the battle; he was away and did not get back till sometime after the battle.[26]

---

[24]If anyone emerges as a hero from the Custer Battle, then it was Captain Frederick W. Benteen whose exemplary determination prevented the Indians from carrying Reno's entrenchments. His conduct was given indirect praise in the findings of the Reno court of inquiry, which concluded that subordinates in some instances did more for the safety of the command by brilliant displays of courage than did Major Reno; Utley, *Chicago Times Account*, p. 468. On June 26, water was obtained by a number of volunteers who later received the coveted Medal of Honor, of which a total of twenty-four were issued to the survivors of the Seventh Cavalry, the greatest number ever awarded for a single armed confrontation; for a list of medal winners, see Melbourne C. Chandler, *Of Garry Owen in Glory* (Annandale, 1960), p. 397.

[25]It is unfortunate that Ruleau was not asked to be more specific as to in which ravine these soldiers had been found. After the Custer battle, rumors were persistent that a number of Custer's troopers had escaped from the battlefield, only to be trapped and slain in a ravine some distance to the east. However, Ruleau's statement may have reference to present Deep Ravine and its branches which contained the bodies of over thirty men. So overwhelming was the stench coming from these decomposing corpses on the bottom that the burials of these men were accomplished by breaking off large clumps of dirt from the edge of the ravine and dropping these onto the bodies below. Many of the men involved in this task took to vomiting, and it stands to reason that some of the bodies at this site may never have received any dirt coverage at all. See Hammer, *Custer in '76*, pp. 116-17; and also Captain Thomas M. McDougall to General Edward S. Godfrey, 5/18/1909, Francis R. Hagner Collection, New York Public Library, which contains his recollections of the burials in Deep Ravine.

[26]Although only a minor chief among the Hunkpapas, Gall's reputation and status among the whites received a considerable boost from his frank interview given on the tenth anniversary of the Custter Battle. Gall explained that his savage behavior during

The chiefs in this battle ranked as follows: Crazy Horse
had command of all the Indians; Gall was next in
precedence, and Knife Chief third. The latter received a
bullet through both arms and his body, breaking both
arms. He lives on the Porcupine abt 8 miles below the
village (near day school 13).[27]

the battle resulted from the killing of his family during Reno's attack. Other Indian
sources fail to mention any casualties among the noncombatants, but contemporary
newspapers disclose the discovery of several slain women and children near the point of
Reno's assault. Gall's status was elevated further by the Indian agent at Standing Rock
who was determined to eradicate the political strength of Sitting Bull; see Graham, *The
Custer Myth*, p. 260; *St. Paul Pioneer Press*, July 18, 1886.

   Born near the forks of the Cheyenne River in 1836, Rain in the Face was one of two
Hunkpapa sons born out of his father's second marriage. Rain's younger brother was
Shave Head, a first sergeant in the Standing Rock Indian Police who was killed in the line
of duty during the arrest of Sitting Bull in 1890. Of Rain's four half brothers, Iron Horn
had risen in social standing and was the chief of a minor Hunkpapa band. In 1873, Rain
was implicated in the killings of two civilians along the Yellowstone. He was arrested by
Captain Thomas W. Custer late in 1875, and brought to Fort Lincoln, from where he
escaped early in 1876, swearing vengeance on the Custers. There are conflicting reports
whether Rain actually participated in the Custer Battle; however, the extreme mutilation
of Tom Custer's body gave rise to immediate speculation about Rain's involvement. His
reputation as Custer's slayer was firmly cemented by the writings of Elizabeth Custer
and Longfellow's poem, "The Revenge of Rain in the Face." He died at his home at
Standing Rock Agency, North Dakota, on September 14, 1905. Eastman, "Rain-in-the-
Face," p. 507; James McLaughlin, *My Friend the Indian* (Seattle, 1970), p. 178; DeCost
Smith, *Indian Experiences* (Caldwell, 1943), pp. 215-247, which contains an excellent
review of this entire matter.

   [27]The wounding of Knife Chief is confirmed by his son Thomas Steals Horses.
Apparently, Knife Chief was shot near Reno's line in the valley, and being so severely
wounded, he remained lying on the battlefield until relatives were able to remove him on
a pony travois. John P. Colhoff to Charles D. Schreiders, 4/30/1943, Agnes W. Spring
Collection, University of Wyoming Heritage Center.

The Flying Hawk Interview

Editorial note: This interview was conducted in 1907 by Eli S. Ricker. The interview resulted in eleven pages of text and one map, recorded in longhand on a tablet in Ricker's handwriting. The following is a verbatim transcript of the microfilm copy of the manuscript.

Moses Flying Hawk
Near Big Bat's
[Pine Ridge Reservation]
March 8, 1907[1]

In interview with him he says:

There [were] at the battle of the Little Big Horn four tribes of Indians, camped there as follows: There were four different camps; there were three camps of Sioux, as follows: Uncpapas, Minneconjous, and Oglalas; also the Cheyennes.[2]

---

[1] One of two sons of Black Fox and Iron Cedar Woman, Flying Hawk was born in an Oglala camp near present Rapid City, South Dakota, in 1852. He was a brother of Kicking Bear, the fanatical leader during the Ghost Dance troubles, and a nephew of the renowned Hunkpapa, Sitting Bull. Flying Hawk passed away at Pine Ridge, South Dakota, on December 24, 1931, its cause rumored to have been starvation. For another account of the Custer Battle by Flying Hawk, see McCreight, *Firewater and Forked Tongues,* pp. 111-116. This present interview is contained in the Eli S. Ricker Collection, Nebraska State Historical Society, reel 3, tablet 13, pp. 40-51.

The extreme length of the camps was about a mile and a half. (I tested this distance and he understands it well.) He says these several bands were camped in large circles; if they had been out in a straight line they would have been as far as from Mestth [?], where we are taking this down, to the White River, a distance of 3½ miles.

He says Custer came down on the second ridge from the river, and he stopped on the high hill above the Indians.[3] About 30 Indians were killed all told. The mutilations of the dead were among Reno's men mostly; a very few of Custer's were mutilated; but there were so many dead that not much of this was done.

All the living men on Custer Hill ran toward the river and were killed by the Indians who were on both sides of the retreating men, killing them with arrows, guns and clubs. This shows that Custer and his officers who fell on Custer Hill were all killed before the soldiers ran for the river.[4] He says that Custer and his men on Custer Hill had their horses with them, but they were dismounted, and as

---

[2] Known to the whites as Sioux, these warlike peoples were divided into three distinct entities, each with their own peculiar dialect. They identified themselves as the Teton Lakotas, the Santee Dakotas, and the Yankton and Yanktonai Nakotas. Royal B. Hassrick, *The Sioux* (Norman, 1964), p. 6. Of the Sioux gathered at the Little Bighorn, the Tetons were most numerous, their population being represented by the seven groups which make up the Lakotas. From their own statements, we know that the Hunkpapa, Minneconjou, and Oglala camps were the largest. The Blackfeet, Brules, Two Kettles and Sans Arcs were represented in much smaller numbers, and their lodges, with the exception of the Sans Arcs, were fused with the larger camps. To illustrate the difference in dialect, I call the reader's attention to the Sioux spelling of Chief Red Top's name, which was known among the Santees as Inkpa *D*uta, and among the Tetons as Inkpa *L*uta.

[3] The "second ridge" is probably the elevated area just east of the present blacktop near Medicine Tail Ford. Viewing this location from the west bank of the river, one sees across the stream a line of perpendicular bluffs which rise some 15 feet above the river's floodplain. The top of the bluffs is fairly level and forms the tableland through which the present blacktop makes a large loop. East of this road, the land rises sharply, its elevation giving the appearance of it being the second ridge back from the river. This latter elevation contains the marker erected for Sergeant James Butler of L Company.

often as the Indians killed one of Custer's men, they took the horse belonging to him; if the horse attempted to escape they caught him. It was only on Custer Hill where the soldiers were surrounded.

On Calhoun Hill, a part of the soldiers stood and gave battle. Custer was at this time on Custer Hill. Finally, the line on Calhoun Hill was broken and the soldiers fell back toward Custer Hill, fighting as they went. A body which corresponds to Keogh's command made a stand on the northeast side of the ridge, and when the most of them were killed the others fell back toward Custer Hill, fighting and falling, and the remnant joined Custer where the living remnant of his command were now surrounded.[5]

Flying Hawk with others left the pursuit of Reno after he had gone to the hills, and as the Indians had some wounded they went down into their camp with the wounded; then they crossed the river and attacked the soldiers on Calhoun Hill. There were also a lot of Indians who had followed the river down from Reno without going to their camp, and these also crossed the river and attacked Calhoun Hill.

Flying Hawk was with the leaders and could see

[4]On June 27, military survivors found the remains of 28 individuals on the bottom of a deep ravine, some 400 yards southwest of Custer Hill. Flying Hawk makes clear that these were the remains of troopers who had failed to gain the safety of the timber along the river at the end of the battle. His narrative refutes the existence of the so-called "south line," a theory which suggests the deployment of E Company at the head of this ravine *at the beginning* of the battle. This theory, widely though incorrectly accepted by scholars and historians alike, was advanced by Charles Kuhlman and expounded in his *Legend into History* (Fort Collins, 1977), pp. 181-89; for a counter view of this invalid theory, see Hardorff, *Markers, Artifacts, and Indian Testimony* (Short Hills, 1985) pp. 54-63. For further refutation, see the Weston interviews with Two Eagles, Lone Bear, Lights, Hollow Horn Bear, and Julia Face, in this volume.

[5]In his account to McCreight, *Firewater and Forked Tongues,* p. 113, Flying Hawk recalled that upon the destruction of Keogh's troop, the remnant fell back to make yet another stand on Custer Ridge, some distance south of the present monument site. It was probably at this location that the Cheyenne, Lame White Man was killed. From this location the survivors withdrew to join the troopers already on Custer Hill.

[everything]. The Indians had crossed the river above Calhoun Hill before Custer left the second ridge. The soldiers saw the Indians down in the creek leading to the river, and then Custer came down off the second ridge and went up onto Calhoun Hill, leaving a detachment there, and he went right on over to Custer Hill and made a stand there. (It is easy to see why he did this from a military point.)

The Sioux and Cheyennes were all mixed up. Some of the Indians crossed from the place the women fled to and went across at the lower crossing west of Custer Hill, and there they caught a lot of soldiers' loose horses, and some of the Indians went up into the fight.[6]

He says Custer did not try to go down to the river by the creek and that there was no fighting on that creek, as others have said. (And no stones have been set there, and I think he is right.)[7]

The man supposed to have been Lt. Harrington was driven back along the ridge with the rest from Calhoun Hill to Custer Hill, and on arriving there he did not stop going, but went right on, and so he knows this man left the field before Custer was killed, because Custer was not yet surrounded. This man fired two shots back, and was seen to fall. He got about half a mile away.[8]

---

[6] The noncombatants were congregated near present Squaw Creek. The lower crossing was at the mouth of Deep Ravine, and since the Cheyennes were camped near this crossing, it has been identified by some scholars as the Cheyenne Ford. After having defended their camp circle, many of the Hunkpapas arrived late at Custer's battlefield. These Hunkpapas crossed at the Cheyenne Ford and ascended the tableland near the foot of Deep Ravine. See DeMallie, *The Sixth Grandfather*, p. 190; for the name use and location of Cheyenne Ford, see Henry and Don Weibert, *Sixty-six Years in Custer's Shadow* (Billings, 1985) pp. 57, 145.

[7] Flying Hawk's reference to Custer being on "the Second ridge" suggests strongly that troops may have come within 300 yards of the river as measured from the elevation. This conclusion is supported by Flying Hawk's kinsman, He Dog, who told Walter Camp in 1910 that Custer's command was scattered along and parallel with the river, and only some 600 feet from it; see Hammer, *Custer in '76*, p. 206.

[8] Listed as missing in action, the whereabouts of Lt. Henry M. Harrington continues to

Flying Hawk thinks that Reno could not get to Custer because they were watched by Indians who would have prevented them, though he does not know how many Indians were watching.[9] The battle began in the morning about 8 or 9 o'clock, and it ended about 1 o'clock p.m., or 2 p.m.[10]

He says that the Indians did not know that Custer was coming; but they had retired with their wounded, and when they passed the creek they saw Custer on the second ridge etc, etc (??).

The fighting was good by the soldiers, especially by those under Reno.[11] He puts the whole Indian loss, including those who died from wounds, at about 30. (?)[12]

----

be a subject of speculation which often unjustly results in implied charges of desertion and cowardice; see, for example, the letter from Edward H. Allison to Judge Eli S. Ricker, 1/21/1906, Allison Correspondence, Nebraska State Historical Society.

[9]Examination of the evidence reveals that the Indians withdrew from Reno's front upon the commencement of the Custer fight. Many scholars have contributed Reno's inactivity on the bluffs to his timidity, indecisiveness, and lack of general leadership abilities. When subordinates no longer could restrain their impatience with Reno's delay, a move was made in Custer's direction by Captain Thomas B. Weir and subsequently by Captain Frederick H. Benteen, the latter ignoring Reno's frantic trumpet signals to abort this move; see Edward C. Baily, "Echoes from Custer's Last Fight," *Military Affairs* (Winter, 1953): 178-79, which contains Lt. Edgerly's account of the circumstances which led to Captain Weir's movement; also, Col. Frederick Benteen to Col. Theodore W. Goldin, March 1, 1892, in John M. Carroll, *The Benteen-Goldin Letters on Custer and His Last Battle* (New York, 1974), p. 215, in which he describes Captain Weir's and his own unauthorized departure.

[10]Flying Hawk confirms the statements made by Respects Nothing and also by Ruleau's informants who all indicated that only three hours passed between the opening of the valley fight and the end of the Custer battle.

[11]This opinion is not shared by a majority of Indian sources who compare Reno's retreat to a wild buffalo stampede, with the Indians of course doing the chasing. This eratic behavior displayed by the troopers seemed to have elicited a number of insulting remarks by the Indians; see Marquis, *Wooden Leg*, p. 221; Stanley Vestal, *Sitting Bull, Champion of the Sioux* (Boston, 1934), p. 164. Of interest also is an interview with the Hunkpapa Lakota, Little Knife, who stated that Reno's retreating soldiers fired wildly over their shoulders, killing some of their own comrades, and that some of the troopers who became unhorsed confronted the Indians with their hands raised in an appeal for pity; see also undated clipping from the *Billings* (Montana) *Gazette*, Billings Clipping File, Billings Public Library.

[12]For a listing of Indian casualties, see the White Bull Interview.

(My own opinion about how they discovered Custer's approach is that Moses Flying Hawk is in error. Frank Feathers and others were over northeast of the river watching ponies. I did not ascertain whether any of these fled to the Indian camp and gave the alarm. But the Indians somehow got notice of the coming of the soldiers.)[13]

The marks made by Moses Flying Hawk on this map, reinforced by his statement at our interview, show that the Indians plunged across the river where the creek empties, in several places, that is, in single file, one successively below the other.

He said that when Custer reached the Custer Hill he was right above the women who had collected down the river, and this is indicated by the map.

---

[13]Ricker's conclusion is supported by the Minneconjou, Standing Bear, who crossed the river to Medicine Tail Coulee to collect his family's ponies. Before he did so, he ascended the elevation now known as Weir Point, from which promontory he saw the advance of both Reno's and Custer's troops. DeMallie, *The Sixth Grandfather*, p. 188.

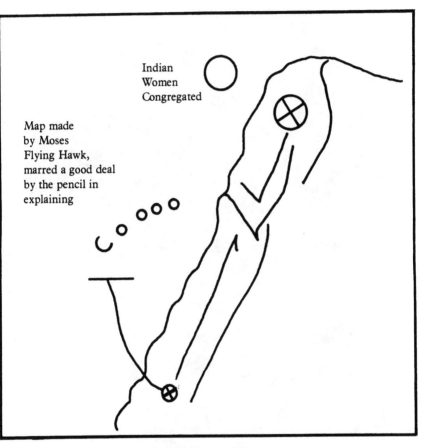

MAP OF FLYING HAWK

THE MINNECONJOU LAKOTA, STANDING BEAR
This picture was taken by Heyn and Matzen of Omaha, Nebraska,
ca. 1900, when Standing Bear was about 41 years old.

The Standing Bear Interview

Editorial note: This interview was conducted in 1907 by Eli S. Ricker. The interview resulted in five pages of text and one map, recorded in longhand on a tablet in Ricker's handwriting. The following is a verbatim transcript of the microfilm copy of the manuscript.

Standing Bear
At Manderson, South Dakota
March 12, 1907[1]

Standing Bear, a full-blooded Sioux Indian, being interpreted, says an Oglala Indian went out on opposite side of the L. Big Horn to look for horses and came back saying that there were white soldiers coming, and then they

---

[1] Standing Bear was a Minneconjou Lakota who was born on Tongue River, Montana, in 1859. In addition to the Ricker interview, Standing Bear also gave a brief account of the Custer Battle to Walter M. Camp in 1910, and a more detailed version to John G. Neihardt in 1931; see Hammer, *Custer in '76*, pp. 214-15; and DeMallie, *The Sixth Grandfather*, pp. 184-89. The present interview is contained in the Eli S. Ricker Collection, Nebraska State Historical Society, reel 3, tablet 13, pp. 55-60. Standing Bear is not to be confused with *Luther* Standing Bear (1863-1936), who was the author of *My People the Sioux* and several other books on Lakota life. Luther was a Brule Lakota of Lip's Wears Salt Band which had settled on Pass Creek on the eastern edge of Pine Ridge Reservation. Luther's father, the elder Standing Bear, was a mixed-blood Brule who remarried among the Oglalas in 1865. He passed away in 1898.

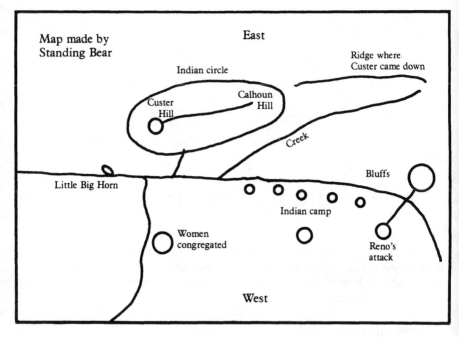

Map made by Standing Bear

East

Indian circle

Ridge where Custer came down

Custer Hill

Calhoun Hill

Creek

Little Big Horn

Bluffs

Indian camp

Women congregated

Reno's attack

West

MAP OF STANDING BEAR

sent out a scout.[2] The Indians saw Custer about noon when he made a charge on them. The first fighting of all the fighting was down on the river bottom and began about noon.[3] He did not fight against Reno. Reno's bullets came

---

[2] This is another reference to the young Lakota named Deeds who accompanied his relative, Brown Back, to the head of Reno Creek in search of a stray pony. Near the divide they became aware of the presence of Custer's troops, and although they both fled the location immediately, only Brown Back reached the village to sound the alarm. After the battle, the slain body of Deeds was found in the brush near the mouth of Reno Creek. There exists a mass of conflicting evidence regarding the true identity and band affiliation of these two individuals, and also regarding the location and circumstances of Deeds' death; see Richard G. Hardorff, "Custer's Trail to Wolf Mountains: A Reevaluation of Evidence," *Custer and His Times: Book Two* (Fort Worth, 1984), pp. 110-113. For additional information on Deeds, see the interview with Moving Robe Woman.

[3] The first fighting has reference to the feeble attack by Major Marcus A. Reno on the southern end of the great village, about 3 p.m. Chicago time.

right into the camp. Standing Bear was in or just back of the camp when Reno attacked it.[4]

Standing Bear says that Custer came down the ridge across the creek—the second or rear ridge from the river. He made no known attempt to reach the river to cross.[5] He went right up to Calhoun Hill and disposed his forces along the top of the ridge to Custer Hill. The men on Calhoun Hill finally gave way and fell back toward Custer Hill. Keogh made a desperate stand and he and his men were killed. The men fell back along the ridge leading their horses. No Indians crossed at the lower crossing. They all crossed at the mouth of the Creek and spread out both ways around Custer, completely encircling his troops and *both hills.*[6]

Custer was first confronted by a few Indians who took position all along the south side of the ridge, and their numbers increased rapidly as the Indians came over the river and joined in battle. There was no fighting on the creek. The soldiers made a stout defense. A good many Indian horses were killed and lying around in the big circle.[7] Twenty-four (24) Indians were all the dead Indians

[4]Although Standing Bear's interview with Walter Camp gives the impression that he was present in the Oglala camp, his statement to Ricker makes clear he was among the Minneconjou lodges just downstream (north) of the Hunkpapas; see Hammer, *Custer in '76* pp. 214, 215.

[5]Mentioned in several other accounts, the "second" or "rear" ridge is the elevation just east of the present blacktop which loops past Medicine Tail Ford on the east bank of the river. His statement that Custer did not attempt to reach the ford is contradicted by his opposite assertion three years later. He then emphasized to Walter Camp that Custer's soldiers had advanced nearly to the river when increased Indian resistance finally succeeded in forcing them back. Hammer, *Custer in '76*, p. 214.

[6]Although Medicine Tail Ford was the principal crossing used, quite a number of the Hunkpapas used the Cheyenne Ford; see DeMallie, *The Sixth Grandfather*, p. 190, which contains Iron Hawk's statement that "the Hunkpapas gathered at the foot of the gulch on the east side of the Little Big Horn that leads up to the Custer hill." Obviously, Iron Hawk described the mouth of Deep Ravine because it was from this location that he observed the stampede of the grey horses and futile escape of the last of Custer's men.

[7]The accuracy of Standing Bear's statement is in doubt, because Captain Frederick W. Benteen attested to having counted only two dead ponies, while Captain Thomas M. McDougall saw five or six. Utley, *The Reno Court of Inquiry: The Chicago Times Account*, p. 327; Hammer, *Custer in '76*, p. 73.

he saw; does not know how many died from wounds. No soldiers were mutilated, either of Custer's or Reno's; but an Indian that was with the soldiers and killed was scalped and cut across the bowels.[8]

The soldiers that fell back along the ridge, uniting with those left alive on Custer Hill, broke and ran on foot down toward the ravine and river and were killed by Indians surrounding them, with arrows, guns and war clubs.[9]

The fight on the river bottom began about noon, and Custer was finished about an hour later. It seemed as though the sun was in the same place when the Custer battle was over, [as] that it was when the Reno fight started.

[8] This reference is to one of the three slain Ree Indians—Bloody Knife, Little Brave, and Bobtail Bull—whose extremely mutilated remains defied identification; Libby, *The Arikara Narrative*, p. 145.

[9] Standing Bear's recollection seems very clear and concise about the sequence of events which led to the deaths of Custer's men found in Deep Ravine. Reliving this last phase of the battle, he told John Neihardt that these soldiers "went into the side of a hill into a draw and there was tall grass in here. We were right on top of the soldiers and there was no use in hiding from us. Then I saw an Indian rush at the men and then the Indians killed every soldier including some of our own Indians who had gone ahead of the rest. When we killed the last man, we could hear the women coming over and it was just a sight with men and horses mixed up together—horses on top of men and men on top of horses." DeMallie, *The Sixth Grandfather*, pp. 186-87. The Custer Battle chapter in the latter publication contains the literal translations of Neihardt's interviews with three elderly Lakotas in 1931. Their statements are rich in details and reveal much information not available in the reworded and abridged previous publication, *Black Elk Speaks*.

THE HUNKPAPA LAKOTA, IRON HAWK
This picture was taken by Heyn and Matzen of Omaha, Nebraska,
ca. 1900, when Iron Hawk was about 38 years old.

The Iron Hawk Interview

Editorial note: This interview was conducted in 1907 by Eli S. Ricker. The interview resulted in twelve pages of text, recorded in longhand on a tablet in Ricker's handwriting. The following is a verbatim transcript of the microfilm copy of the manuscript.

Iron Hawk
Chadron, Nebraska
[May 13] 1907[1]

The Indian tribes who fought Custer were Oglalas, Cheyennes, Rosebud or Brule, Minneconjous, Uncpapas, Santee, a few Arapahoes, and Sans Arcs or No Bows (Itazi Pco, pronounced Etahz Pcho.) The Indians were camped on the Little Big Horn two nights before the Custer battle which began on the third day in the morning.[2] The battle began early, about 8 or 9 o'clock, judging from the position of the sun as shown by Iron Hawk.

Two young men were going back on the Indian trail

---

[1] Iron Hawk was a Hunkpapa Lakota who was born in Montana in 1862. For a lengthier account of the Custer Battle, see his interview in DeMallie, *The Sixth Grandfather*, pp. 190-93. The Iron Hawk interview is contained in the Ricker Collection, Nebraska State Historical Society, reel 5, tablet 25, pp. 131-42.

toward the east looking for ponies, and they discovered the troops coming. One of these boys was killed. The other returned to the camp and gave the alarm, and the camp was thrown in the utmost confusion.[3] The Uncpapas were in the upper camp up the river. Soon the soldiers were seen in line of battle with their flags displayed, their staffs being planted in the ground, and then the firing began.[4] The soldiers could not be seen, but the smoke of their fire was plain. They were in the point of timber. His [Reno's] troops did not get into the camp among the teepees. They did not advance beyond the timber. He says the soldiers were in the timber but a short time.

Iron Hawk was busy from the start arousing the warriors to duty and hurrying them to mount their horses in readiness to defend the camp. These braves were collecting on the flank of the soldiers close to the high bank which borders the river bottom on the west.[5] Presently, Crazy Horse, having collected his warriors, made a dash for the soldiers in the timber and ran into them; when the warriors assembling close to the bank saw this movement and heard

---

[2] Iron Hawk makes clear that the great village on the Little Bighorn was erected on June 23, which date was positively confirmed by the Oglala, Knife, who courted his wife in the valley on the 23rd, and he eloped with her on the 24th, the time and romantic interlude firmly implanted on his memory; see Blish, *A Pictographic History of the Oglala Sioux*, p. 197. Some sources suggest that the village may not have been established until June 24, which contradiction is perhaps due to the fact that on the latter date several small bands joined the great encampment; see Hammer, *Custer in '76*, pp. 198, 201.

[3] A clear reference to Deeds and his slaying.

[4] This was Major Reno's command of Companies A, M, and G which deployed in skirmish order across the valley near the present Garryowen bend.

[5] Iron Hawk's party had collected below the high bank of the dry river channel just north (downstream) of Reno's position in the woods. Eventually, these Indians filtered into the brush behind Reno's line and they may have fired the volley which killed several of Reno's men. See DeMallie, *The Sixth Grandfather*, p. 182, which contains the recollections of the Oglala, Black Elk, who had followed his older brother to this point. See also Hammer, *Custer in '76*, p. 223, and Graham, *The Custer Myth*, pp. 258, 263, which contain the observations by George Herendeen who witnessed this volley at close range.

the yells of Crazy Horse's men they also advanced furiously with great yelling, coming down on the flank.[6] The soldiers broke and ran in retreat, the Indians using war clubs as the principal weapon, a few using bows and arrows, most of the execution being by knocking the troopers from their horses, the Indians moving right in among them.

The Uncpapas were the first Indians reached when Reno began his attack. Iron Hawk says the Indians were so thick that Reno's men would have been run over and could not have lasted but a short time if they had stood their ground in the woods.

All the Indians said another lot of soldiers are moving down on the other side of the ridge.[7] They all made a rush and got across the river. At one end of the attacking Indians was Sitting Bull, and at the other end was Crazy Horse. (He is not sure about Sitting Bull, but thinks he was in the fight. Says there were so many Indians that there was no telling about many things.)[8] About 19 Indians were killed. Others

---

[6] Arriving late at the valley fight, Crazy Horse's presence gave renewed vigor to the Indian attack which drove Reno's disorganized command from the valley floor; see McCreight, *Firewater and Forked Tongues,* p. 112; DeMallie, *The Sixth Grandfather,* p. 182. According to Standing Bear, the valor displayed by Crazy Horse during this phase of the battle was spoken of by all the people.

[7] The "other lot of soldiers" was Custer's command of five companies.

[8] Sitting Bull was a ranked member of the Strong Hearts Society and the spiritual leader of the Hunkpapa Lakotas. He was born on the Grand River near the present town of Bullhead, South Dakota, in 1831, near which location he was killed while resisting arrest on December 15, 1890. For his biography, see Stanley Vestal, *Sitting Bull, Champion of the Sioux* (Boston, 1932); and also Stanley Vestal, *New Sources of Indian History 1850-1891* (Norman, 1934); John M. Carroll, *The Arrest and Killing of Sitting Bull: A Documentary* (Glendale, 1987). By request of his direct descendants, Sitting Bull's remains were exhumed from the Fort Yates Cemetery, North Dakota, on April 8, 1953, and reinterred that same day near Mobridge, South Dakota. This exhumation released an angry exchange of charges and counter charges between both states regarding the jurisdiction over the remains and the legality of this transfer across state lines, its feud eventually resolved by the federal authorities. For an entertaining volume on this matter, see Robb DeWall, *The Saga of Sitting Bull's Bones* (Crazy Horse, S.D., 1984).

were wounded, but how many he does not know. The soldiers were stripped but not mutilated.

Thinks Sitting Bull was at one end of the attacking Indians, Crazy Horse at one end, and Iron Hawk was on the side toward the ridge and between the ridge and the river in the attack on Custer.[9] They surrounded Custer.

Says Custer's men in the beginning shot straight, but later they shot like drunken men, firing into the ground, into the air, wildly in every way. Where Custer fell there were about 20 on horseback and about 30 on foot.[10] The Indians pressed and crowded right in around them on Custer Hill; one [soldier] broke through on horseback and got away, [and] Indians followed, [but] Iron Hawk told them to let him go and tell the story; he outstripped them, but he dismounted after riding about three quarters of a

---

[9] Iron Hawk was positioned near the forks of Deep Ravine, southwest of Custer Hill, where he participated in the final stages of the battle.

[10] A body count of the slain on Custer Hill revealed the remains of ten individuals on the crest, while some thirty-two bodies were found on its southwestern slope. Initially as many as ninety troopers may have occupied this elevation. See, for example, the account by the Cheyenne, Two Moons, who stated that near the end of the battle some forty-five men left the hill in an attempt to reach the woods along the river; see Graham, *The Custer Myth*, p. 103. The crest of Custer Hill was a nearly level place of some 30 feet in diameter. Six sorrel horses had been slain around its perimeter, the color identifying them as belonging to Company C. General George Custer was found near the southwestern edge of the elevation, behind a horse, his right leg across the body of a soldier, while his back was slumped against the bodies of two others. The latter two were identified as probably being Sergeant John Vickory, the regimental color bearer, who lay with his face up. The second body was identified as that of Chief Trumpeter Henry Voss, who lay across Vickory's head, Voss' face being down. Vickory had his right arm cut off at the shoulder. Some 20 feet back from Custer, toward the east side of this level place, lay the extemely mutilated body of Captain Tom Custer. He was laying on his face, the skull broken and flattened from repeated blows to the head. Lt. William W. Cooke, his thighs slashed and one of the black whiskers scalped, was found between two horses, close to Tom. The fourth officer on the crest was Lt. Algernon E. Smith, his body having been riddled with arrows. Of the remaining four enlistees, the names of only two are known—Privates John Parker and Edward C. Driscoll, both of Company I, whose bodies lay near the eastern edge of the elevation; see Richard G. Hardorff, *The Custer Battle Casualties: Burials, Exhumations and Reinterments* (El Segundo, 1989), pp. 33-35.

mile and shot himself in the forehead. He would have escaped.[11]

When Custer was retreating toward Custer Hill, Indians followed along picking up arms and revolvers and ammunition and went to using these instead of clubs and bows and arrows. From Custer Hill a lot of soldiers broke and ran toward the river when the Indians pressed in on them, and they were killled in trying to escape.[12] Two men on this hill wore buckskin suits; another wore such suit at the other end, which means Calhoun Hill.[13]

Iron Hawk was wounded in the battle, shot through the body; he showed me the wound, the bullet passing through from one side below the ribs and slanting upwards [it] went nearly through but did not come out on the other side.

He did not go over the field after the battle. He knew ' Rain-in-the-Face and he says he was in the fight. He says

[11]Yet another reference to an attempted escape, this one occurring near the end of the battle, from Custer Hill. Although the evidence is at variance, this individual may have been Corporal John Foley of C Company whose body was found on a little elevation along Medicine Tail Coulee, some 300 yards east from the river. See Hammer, *Custer in '76*, pp. 206, 254; Camp Manuscripts, p. 559, Indiana University Library.

[12]For a graphic description of this final phase of the battle, see Iron Hawk's frank interview in DeMallie, *The Sixth Grandfather*, pp. 191-92, which contains his vivid recollections of the killings in and around Deep Ravine.

[13]Having learned the identity of their white adversaries several weeks later, many Indians formed the conclusion that General Custer must have been one of the buckskin clad men slain on the hill. One Indian, Standing Bear, had taken a buckskin jacket from one of the dead men which he gave to his mother, and for many years they supposed it was Custer's jacket. This garment was kept hidden until his mother finally cut it up and disposed of it for fear of being caught with incriminating evidence. The Indians' conception of a Custer fully clad in buckskin has been perpetuated through the artistic renditions of many artists. This visualization seemed to have gained acceptance among a number of scholars. However, a careful scrutiny of the present evidence seems to suggest the opposite to be true. Custer may have worn a buckskin outfit on June 25, but so did both of his slain brothers, while at least five other officers who fell with him may have worn a buckskin jacket. It is true that a melancholy reflection by Custer's longtime orderly, John Burkman, reveals an image of Custer wearing a white hat, fringed buckskin coat, and a red tie while galloping away at noon, June 25. But sequential evidence about Custer's apparel seems to suggest a different picture. One source of evidence is provided

the whole nation was in the fight; he seems to argue from this that Rain-in-the-Face was there.

Iron Hawk has a silver medal with the image of Pres. Grant on one side and these words: "United States of America. Liberty, Justice and Equality. Let us have Peace." On the reverse side is the open Holy Bible, a globe with the words on opposite side of the globe: "Atlantic Ocean", "Pacific Ocean", a stump, plow rake, hoe, shovel, axe, and these words and figures: "On Earth Peace, Goodwill Toward Men. 1871". The medal is about 2½ inches in diameter and some ³⁄₁₆ of an inch thick.

Iron Hawk says the Indians crossed the river anywhere to confront Custer. The first Indians to reach Custer were about one hundred (100).[14] He says Custer did not get anywhere near the river; his nearest approach was about a mile off. It must have been about three fourths of a mile at least.[15] He remembers that Keogh and his men were killed

---

by the Ree Scout, Soldier, who told Walter Camp that Custer took off his buckskin coat and tied it behind his saddle. There can be no doubt that this observation was made hours after Burkman's because it occurred near the lower forks of Reno Creek. The validity of Soldier's statement receives a boost from Lt. Charles A. DeRudio, who attested to having seen both General Custer and Lt. Cook near Reno Hill, the identification made possible through their clothing—a blue shirt and buckskin pants—the only officers to wear such a combination. Moreover, Peter Thompson, a survivor of Company C, gained his last view of Custer north of Reno Hill, and he described Custer as an alert man, dressed in a shirt, buckskin pants tucked in his boots , and buckskin jacket fastened to the rear of his saddle. Although Thompson embellished considerably on his recollections, the essence of this observation does not involve a selfserving matter. We may therefore conclude from these corroborating sources that the clothing pillaged from Custer's body consisted of a blue shirt and fringed buckskin pants, and that the man fully clad in buckskin was either Boston Custer or his brother, Captain Tom; see Graham, *The Custer Myth*, p. 345; Glendolin D. Wagner, *Old Neutriment* (New York, 1973), pp. 151, 155; Hammer, *Custer in '76*, p. 188; Graham, *Abstract of the Reno Court of Inquiry*, p. 115; and Daniel O. Magnussen, *Peter Thompson's Narrative of the Little Bighorn Campaign, 1876* (Glendale, 1974), pp. 145-46.

[14] The initial force which blocked Custer's progress at Medicine Tail Ford consisted of some ten to twenty Indians, four of whom were Cheyennes; see Hammer, *Custer in '76*, p. 207; Grinnell, *The Fighting Cheyennes*, pp. 350, 357; Stanley Vestal, *Warpath and Council Fire* (New York, 1948), p. 245.

near the little ravine.[16] Iron Hawk was on the field between the ridge and the river.

The foregoing interview was on Sunday, May 13th, in the tent of Archie Sword, son of the brother of Captain George Sword, at Chadron.[17] Archie Sword is a son-in-law of Iron Hawk. He is a freight handler at the depot.

Iron Hawk's discription of the Custer Battle was in the sign language, graphic in the extreme. He is a large,

---

[15]Although this statement is supported by others, notably the Hunkpapa, Gall, there is opposing and more convincing evidence that some of Custer's men came close enough to the river to fire into and over the teepees on the other side. See, for example, the statement by the Oglala, Foolish Elk, in Hammer, *Custer in '76*, p. 198, and also that by the Hunkpapa, Good Voiced Elk, in Walter Mason Camp Papers, Item 6, Denver Public Library. For an analysis of the evidence, see Hardorff, *Markers, Artifacts and Indian Testimony*, pp. 24-28.

[16]As a result of rank seniority, Captain Myles W. Keogh commanded Companies I, L, and C in the Custer Battle. On June 27, the remains of Captain Keogh and his immediate command—principally I Company and a few men from L and C—were discovered on the eastern slope of Custer Ridge, near the head of a narrow ravine. Keogh's remains were found in an old buffalo wallow. Across his breast lay the body of his trumpeter, John W. Patton, while near him were found Sergeants James Bustard and Frank E. Varden, both of Company I. Keogh's body did not reveal any signs of mutilation. Comtemporary observers concluded that he had been crippled by a gunshot wound which extensively fractured his left knee and leg. Death came later as his trumpeter and non-commissioned staff chose to remain with him to the end. See Walter Camp Manuscripts, pp. 32, 106, Indiana University Library; Richard G. Hardorff, "Captain Keogh's Insurance Policy," *Research Review* (September, 1977):17.

[17]Also known as Hunts the Enemy, Owns Sword was the son of the Oglala, Brave Bear, of the Bad Face Band. Sword later took the Christian name of George. He was an exceptionally brave and intelligent individual whose leadership abilities led to his election to the office of Shirt Wearer in the late 1860s. The fact that his uncle was Chief Red Cloud may have contributed to Sword's political aspirations and success. Sword twice visited Washington as a member of the Oglala delegations, and perhaps as a result of these visits, he became a "progressive" leader at an early age, realizing that acceptance of the ways of the whites was inevitable. An emissary for the U.S. Military, Sword was instrumental in the negotiations in 1877 which led to the surrender of the renowned Crazy Horse. Three years later, he accepted the position of Captain of the Pine Ridge Indian Police, and in this capacity he faithfully served the U.S. Government for many years. His devotion to his office and Indian Agent Valentine McGillycuddy led at times to friction with Chief Red Cloud, especially during the Ghost Dance troubles of the late 1880s. On a humanitarian note, Sword adopted a little girl who was found alive on the frozen battlefield of Wounded Knee in 1890. He died of natural causes near Chadron, Nebraska, the date unknown to me.

powerful man, features strong and typical, pleasing face, [and] grave demeaner which gives way to great animation when he reaches interesting discourse.

Iron Hawk says that the sun was at the meridian when the Custer battle was all over. He looked at the sun when all were killed. Iron Hawk's language in expressing the time was that the sun was "in the middle" of the sky when he looked up. When the fighting began under Reno, Iron Hawk's gestures indicated it was 8 or 9 o'clock.

THE OGLALA LAKOTA, HE DOG (1840-1936)
This picture was taken by an unidentified photographer in Washington
D.C., 1877, when He Dog was about 37 years old.
Courtesy of the West Point Military Academy.

The He Dog Interview

Editorial note: This interview was conducted in 1919 by Gen. Hugh L. Scott during his inspection tour of the Indian reservations as an appointed member of the Board of Indian Affairs. This interview resulted in eight letter-size pages of text, recorded in longhand, apparently in Scott's handwriting. The translations were probably provided by Baptiste Pourier and William Garnett who were present during this interview, and who were both fluent in the Lakota language. The following is a verbatim transcript of the original manuscript.

He Dog
Pine Ridge Agency
[August 19, 1920][1]

He Dog, Red Feather, and Whirling were asked if they were in the Custer fight and said they were, all of them. Red

---

[1] The son of Black Rock and Blue Day Woman, He Dog was born in 1840 in Old Smoke's Oglala camp near Bear Butte, South Dakota. Blue Day belonged to the powerful Smoke family which was led by her brother, Old Smoke. Her sisters were Walks as She Thinks and Bega. The latter's son, Spotted Bear, was better known as Bad Face, the name by which the Smoke Band became known. He Dog excelled in martial skills, and the pictographs of his nephew, Amos Bad Heart Bull, testify to He Dog's war exploits with frequency. But in addition to his warrior skills, he also exhibited leadership abilities, and as a result of these qualities, He Dog was elected to the office of Shirt Wearer in the late 1860s. Called "Owners of the Tribe," these outstanding men were entrusted with the

Feather (now policeman) said he attacked Reno and went up to the hill where he saw the pack mules, and came back toward the village. Part way, he met _____ with broken leg and helped to fix his leg.[2] Just then word was brought that soldiers were going to attack the lower end of the village, and he went there and took part in the fight.

He Dog left the Hunkpapa village and went to "X" on the map and fought there with Custer.[3] The alarm was given first that soldiers were coming below, by women who had been out on the north side of the river (Greasy Grass = Little Big Horn), digging turnips. They could see the dust and were certain they were soldiers.[4] There was great confusion everywhere, and most of the women and children stampeded to the bluff, marked "ridge" on the map.[5]

---

difficult responsibilities to govern the Oglalas through unstable times. By 1870, a second honor was bestowed upon He Dog. In recognition of his indisputed valor and character, the powerful class of warriors elected him to lead the military lodge of the Crow Owners. Thus, the next six years, he not only fought enemy tribes, but he also resisted white encroachment, culminating in 1876 with the Indian victory at the Little Bighorn. However, He Dog realized that further resistance to the whites was futile, and on May 6, 1877, he and his band surrendered to the U.S. Military at Fort Robinson, Nebraska. Although reservation life was stifling to him, He Dog did become a "progressive" leader. His high moral standards and leadership abilities earned him the position of judge to the Court of Indian Offenses in the 1890s. He served this post for many years until advanced age and failing sight made further service impossible. It was said he was a living depository of Oglala tribal history and old-time customs—one whose knowledge was eagerly sought by such notables as George Hyde, Helen Blish, and Mari Sandoz. He Dog passed away in 1936. This present interview is contained in the Hugh L. Scott Collection, Smithsonian Institution, box 3, item 2932. For another account by He Dog, see Hammer, *Custer in '76*, pp. 203-208.

The Lakota, Whirling, has not been positively identified. For biographical data on Red Feather, see the next interview.

[2] The manuscript does not reveal the name of this Lakota individual.

[3] The He Dog interview does not contain a map. However, there is a map appended to the Red Feather interview, but a careful examination fails to disclose any such contextual marking. Apparently, the He Dog map is missing.

[4] While on the northeast side of the river, one of these Sioux women detected the dust kicked up by a squad of six troopers near Luce Ridge, this squad being well in advance of Custer's column. See Walter Camp to Gen. Edward S. Godfrey, 5/28/1923, Francis R. Hagner Collection, New York Public Library.

Custer was coming from the north, across the dry creek (Custer Creek), and He Dog was among those who attacked him near the dry creek. Custer never got near the river.[6] The troops were in line of small columns, and they made six companies and were galloping. They stopped along the ridge, the side of the ridge away from the river, and the Sioux on opposite side of same ridge, as far apart as to that flagpole (40 yards).[7]

Stretched along the ridge (on which is the monument now), there is a sort of gap in the ridge which Crazy Horse broke thru, cutting the line in two. The fighting was going on everywhere. Now and then a horse would break loose and run down river, and Indians would catch them up. The part of the line cut off fought their way to the others at the end of the ridge.[8] Some of the soldiers got away toward the river, but were all killed.[9]

One soldier with a stocking-legged horse got away, around the big body of Indians, toward the north. He had a

[5] Most of the noncombatants fled downstream to seek shelter in present Squaw Creek, which they ascended when they learned to their horror of Custer's approach across the river. See also the map appended to the Red Feather interview.

[6] The dry creek referred to by He Dog, and identified by Scott as Custer Creek, is the present Medicine Tail Coulee, known by most Lakotas as Water Rat Creek. Although Custer's command consisted of only five companies, one of these may have been divided into two platoons. In 1910, He Dog told Walter Camp that Custer's troops near Medicine Tail Coulee were moving parallel with the river, and only a few hundred yards from it; see Hammer, *Custer in '76*, pp. 206-207.

[7] In the sequence of events, He Dog fails to mention the combat action which took place on Calhoun Ridge.

[8] The gap spoken of can barely be seen due to the geographical changes made in the hillocks in 1932 to provide for a blacktop on Custer Ridge. The combat action at this location centers around I Company which was trapped and annihilated.

[9] The present markers between Custer Hill and Deep Ravine indicate the probable *path* of these fleeing soldiers. Although these stones convey the impression of being kill sites, less than a dozen bodies were found along this route, while an additional 28 bodies were found on the bottom of Deep Ravine. The current placement of these markers has caused erroneous impressions to visitors and researchers alike, resulting in the now generally accepted theory of a combat line near Deep Ravine early in the battle, while in fact none of this is true; see Hardorff, *Markers, Artifacts, and Indian Testimony*, pp. 54-63.

very fast horse and was pursued until they were about to give up the chase, when he shot himself with his revolver and the horse was caught. (This was thought to have been Harrington. He Dog says he [the soldier] was beating the horse with the revolver and was yelling away. He fired backward now and then. He thinks the revolver went off accidently in the beating of the horse; on the other hand, they say that this was his last cartridge.)[10]

He Dog says it was about two hours from Reno's attack until all was over. The next day a man had a telescope and saw troops coming up the river. He Dog had a glass and saw them also.[11] Lame Deer went through all the villages, urging them to move away. They did so. He Dog went to his lodge. His family had run off, leaving the lodge standing. He followed them up and overtook some wounded men and told them the soldiers (Terry) had gone into camp.[12]

They [the Indians] went up Greasy Grass Creek (Little Horn) to the mountains and staid [sic] there two weeks; then over to Tongue River and staid there two weeks. While there, some Cheyennes chased some soldiers into the mountains and got all their horses. (Sibley, 2nd Cav[alry], and Frank Grouard.) Bat lost his horse there—he will tell you about it.[13]

---

[10]The pictographs of Bad Heart Bull, a nephew of He Dog who was his informant, may well portray the flight and kill site of this trooper. See Blish, *A Pictographic History of the Oglala Sioux,* pp. 256-57; 269-72.

[11]This was Gen. Alfred H. Terry with the Montana Column, which went into bivouac June 26, near the present site of Crow Agency, Montana, only a few miles north of Custer's battlefield.

[12]Lame Deer was a Minneconjou leader who was killed by troops under Gen. Nelson A. Miles on present Lame Deer Creek, Montana, May 7, 1877. After the battle, one of Lame Deer's three surviving sons, Flying By, returned to recover his father's body, but found it decapitated, the trunk containing 17 bullet wounds. A search for the missing head was made in vain, and Flying By assumed it had been carried off by the troops as a trophy. For an excellent review of this minor engagement, see Jerome A. Greene, "The Lame Deer Fight: Last Drama of the Sioux War of 1876-1877," *By Valor and Arms* (No. 3, 1978): 11-21.

While He Dog was talking in words, Red Feather was behind the interpreter, making signs that the Indians were scared. They had killed a lot of soldiers and were running off so they would not have to account for it. He Dog said he did not know Custer had been killed for two weeks when a Missouri River Sioux brought out the news. He and Red Feather agreed that the Sioux thought the soldiers with Reno and Custer were Crook's command,[14] and they did not know anything about Custer being in that country until afterward. They say Custer never got any nearer to the river than the monument. Only a few soldiers who broke away were killed below toward the river.[15]

Talking afterward, He Dog asked why Custer attacked without sending someone to talk to them first, and confirmed what the Minneconjou, Feather Earring, at Poplar River said last summer—that they could have been led into the agency without a fight, by some fearless messenger, saying, we, e.g. Crazy Horse and himself, went in when Red Cloud came out and told them to come in the next spring.[16] The Indian view of the matter is that they were living on their own ground, making their living hunting buffalo as they had always done. The soldiers came out and attacked them (Little Powder), then again on the

---

[13]After a gallant little fight with Cheyennes, Sibley's party escaped by abandoning their horses in the woods. The only casualty was the Cheyenne, White Antelope, whose body was carried off by the Indians, who were unaware of the abandoned horses. The next morning, however, a hunting party of Hunkpapas discovered the horses in the brush and found plenty of ammunition in the saddlebags. According to Has Horns, these were exceptionally fine horses who were used to run races against those captured in the Custer fight. Walter Camp Manuscripts, Indiana University Library, p. 356. The individual referred to as Bat is Baptiste Pourier.

[14]General George Crook, whose command was engaged by these same Indians along the Rosebud, Montana, on June 17, 1876.

[15]He Dog's statement is incorrect. Judging from the physical evidence of military casings and skeleton remains, as many as eight troopers may have held a position at the west end of Calhoun Ridge, on top of the cutbank near the mouth of Deep Coulee; see Hardorff, *Markers, Artifacts, and Indian Testimony,* pp. 41-42.

Rosebud, and the third time on the Little Horn. Those Santees and other Indians had come out to hunt buffalo and not to fight, and the Sioux only fought when attacked.[17]

He Dog had a conference some time ago with an officer [acquainted] with Mrs. [Elizabeth B.] Custer, and [He Dog] wanted to know what they were after—were they trying to get paid for [the] killing [of] these soldiers? It was explained that all with Custer had been killed and no one could tell what happened. There were many disputes in consequence, and Mrs. Custer was only trying to settle some of these disputes. He Dog said he had told the officer if he wanted to know the cause of that trouble, he would have to look in Washington—Custer did not come out

[16]Promised greater political influence over the Oglalas, Red Cloud accepted a mission from the U.S. Military to persuade Crazy Horse and his band to surrender. Accomplishing his objective through the efforts of his nephew, Owns Sword, the hostiles were escorted to Camp Robinson by Red Cloud personally, the surrender taking place on May 6, 1877; see Harry H. Anderson, "Indian Peace-Talkers and the Conclusion of the Sioux War of 1876," *Nebraska History* (December, 1963): 233-54.

Born east of the Black Hills in 1821, Red Cloud was the dominant leader of the Bad Face Band of the Oglalas. He is perhaps best known for his determined resistance against the establishments of forts on the Bozeman Trail along the eastern slope of the Big Horn Mountains. Rightfully named Red Cloud's War, the hostilities culminated in the Fetterman Battle of December 21, 1866, and led to the abandonment of these military posts two years later. For biographical data on Red Cloud, see George Hyde, *Red Cloud's Folk* (Norman, 1937), and also James C. Olson, *Red Cloud and the Sioux Problem* (Lincoln, 1965).

Feather Earring was a Minneconjou Lakota who came from a long line of respected ancestors, often mentioned in the Lakota winter counts. For his account of the Custer Battle, see Graham, *The Custer Myth*, pp. 97-98.

[17]Having found sanctuary in Canada after the Sioux uprising of 1862, some twenty lodges of Santee Dakotas under old Red Top came south from Manitoba and joined the Tetons in the fall of 1875. One of these Santees was White Foot Print, who was the uncle of Charles Eastman, the agency physician at Pine Ridge; see Dr. Charles Eastman, "The Story of the Little Big Horn, *Chautaugan* (July, 1900): 353, 354.

The engagements referred to by He Dog took place on March 17, 1876, when Colonel Joseph J. Reynolds attacked a Cheyenne village on the Powder River (He Dog was present with ten lodges of Oglalas, he personally losing seven prized ponies.); June 17, 1876, when the battle of the Rosebud took place between General George Crook and Sioux and Cheyenne forces; June 25, 1876, when General Custer attacked these same Indian forces at the Little Bighorn.

himself; someone there gave him orders and he had to come; that Washington was the place all those troubles started.[18]

He Dog said there were 2000 lodges.[19] When asked if Custer and Reno had kept together and charged down on the village from up the Little Horn bottom, would they in his opinion have succeeded, he replied that there were too many Sioux there. They could not have succeeded no matter what they did.

He Dog stated that he and Crazy Horse moved down to Fort Robinson from the Powder when Red Cloud had come out and told them to come in to the Agency. There was an officer and some scouts [who] came out to them not far from Hat Creek, and Crazy Horse would not speak to him, and he returned. Lt. Clark met him near the Agency and Crazy Horse shook hands with him. He Dog dressed Clark in his war clothes—warbonnet, war shirt, and pipe. He pointed the pipe to the sun and made the Indian prayer: "I gave him my war clothes, my gun, and my horse in token that I would fight no more."[20]

---

[18] The emotional pain of her husband's passing prohibited Elizabeth B. Custer from ever visiting his battlefield, or, for that matter, inquiring into the agonizing details of his death. Mrs. Custer never visited Pine Ridge Agency.

[19] In 1910, He Dog told Walter Camp that the Hunkpapas were the most numerous of all the bands represented at the Little Bighorn; that the combined total of the Hunkpapa and Blackfoot lodges was around 600; that the Minneconjou circle was next in size; and that the whole village consisted of some 1800 lodges; Hammer, *Custer in '76*, p. 206.

[20] On May 2, 1877, Lt. J. Wesley Rosenquest, Fourth Cavalry, and a small detachment were dispatched from Camp Robinson to carry rations to Crazy Horse, the latter refusing to shake hands with him. However, on May 6, Lt. William P. Clark, Second Cavalry, and a detachment of twenty Indian Scouts met Crazy Horse about 5 miles west from Camp Robinson and accepted his surrender. Although he shook hands with Clark, Crazy Horse said defiantly, "I have given all I have to Red Cloud," probably meaning he had surrendered to the old Oglala chief, but *not* to the U.S. Military; see Oliver Knight, "War or Peace: The Anxious Wait for Crazy Horse," *Nebraska History* (Winter, 1973): 540; and also Carroll Friswold, and Robert A. Clark, *The Killing of Chief Crazy Horse, Three Eyewitness Views*, (Glendale, 1976), pp. 49-68, which contains He Dog's lengthy narrative account of the surrender and death of Crazy Horse.

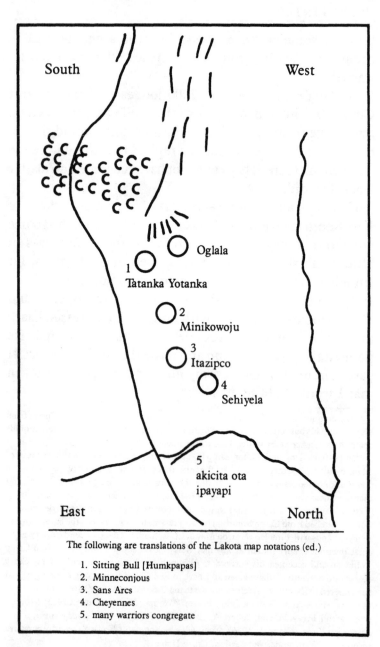

The following are translations of the Lakota map notations (ed.)

1. Sitting Bull [Humkpapas]
2. Minneconjous
3. Sans Arcs
4. Cheyennes
5. many warriors congregate

MAP OF RED FEATHER

The Red Feather Interview

Editorial note: This interview was conducted in 1919 by Gen. Hugh L. Scott during his inspection tour of the Indian reservations as an appointed member of the Board of Indian Affairs. This interview resulted in eight letter-size pages of text and one map, recorded in longhand on a notepad, apparently in Scott's handwriting. The translations were probably provided by Baptiste Pourier and William Garnett who were present during the interview, and who were both fluent in the Lakota language. The following is a verbatim transcript of the original manuscript.

Red Feather
Pine Ridge Agency
[August 19, 1920)[1]

Red Feather had been up very late. He had been dancing and was after the girls. Went hard to sleep. Wakened later to hear some woman say, "You young men take the horses to pasture." Later on he heard someone say, "Go get horses—buffaloes are stampeding!"[2] Magpie came dashing in with the horses, shouting, "Get away as fast as you can, don't wait for anything, the white men are charging!" Just as Red Feather was getting up, the shooting commenced. He saw the soldiers on foot shooting at Sitting Bull's camp. The people in Sitting Bull's camp ran to the Oglala camp. The Oglalas ran, too.[3]

The Indians were catching their ponies and running to the bluff-hills near there. When Red Feather was putting his bridle on his pony, Crazy Horse came out with his bridle and rifle, and said to Red Feather, "Our ponies aren't in yet." Red Feather said, "Take any horse." Red Feather had his horse ready, so he followed the others onto the hill. The hill was covered with men, warriors congregating from the Oglala and Uncpapa camps; the other camps were now in commotion.[4] The sun was quite well up.

The warriors were on horseback, while the women and children were on foot, running to the hill. Red Feather said, "Why wait for the women and children to get tired. Come on!" and started down the hill. [They] charged toward the soldiers; there were two places where flags were

---

[1]Red Feather was an Oglala Lakota and a member of Big Road's band of Northern Oglalas. In 1870, Red Feather's sister, Black Shawl Woman, became the wife of Crazy Horse, and as a result he and Red Feather became close associates. After the surrender in 1877, Red Feather gave his support to the white authorities, and he rendered valuable services during the turbulent times of the Ghost Dance troubles. In later years, he became a devout Catholic. He was a member of the Pine Ridge Indian Police until an amputation of his leg made further service impossible. Red Feather was described by one contemporary as being a shrewd judge of character and a skillful diplomat. The year of his death is unknown to me. This interview is contained in the Hugh L. Scott Collection, Smithsonian Institution, box 4, item 4525.

[2]The dust thrown up by Custer's column was mistaken by some of the Indians for the approach of a buffalo herd. Earlier a single buffalo was killed along Reno Creek by a lone Lakota hunter, who abandoned his kill upon the approach of the troops. This hunter returned to the village in a roundabout way and arrived too late to give the alarm. The discovery of the abandoned buffalo cadaver increased Custer's apprehension that the Indians had discovered him and had commenced to scatter. See Graham, *The Custer Myth*, pp. 60, 61; McLaughlin, *My Friend the Indian*, p. 44; Hammer, *Custer in '76*, pp. 84, 204.

[3]On the appended map, Red Feather locates the Oglala circle adjacent to the Hunkpapas. However, most Indian recollections place the Ogalala lodges near the Cheyennes, on the northwestern end of the great village, but nearer the foothills.

[4]The hill spoken of is situated west of Garryowen, the vantage point being just south of present Shoulder Blade Creek, known to the old-time Sioux as Box Elder Creek; see also General Nelson A. Miles, *Personal Recollections* (New York, 1897), p. 286, who was shown this location during his visit in 1878.

planted, and it was toward these they charged. As the Indians charged, the soldiers took down their flags and started to retreat toward the woods back of them. The Indians who couldn't catch their horses went in the woods on the side of the soldiers and shot at them from the side—not the back, [but] from the side.[5]

One flag bearer was shot down but sat up again. Red Feather was in front and hit him with his quirt. The man behind took the flag away from the soldier.[6] When the soldiers got on their horses, it would have been wise if they had stayed in the woods and shoot [sic] from there. Two soldiers tried to get away, but the Indians overtook and killed them. There was dust around the woods.[7]

Some Indian shouted, "Give way; let the soldiers out. We can't get at them in there." Soon the soldiers came out and tried to go to the river. When they came out of the woods, they were excited and scattered, the Indians mixed with them. Just then Crazy Horse came; his horses were

[5] These Indians eventually fired a point-blank volley at Reno's assembled troops in the clearing, mortally wounding Troopers Henry Klotzbucher and George Lorentz, both of M Company, and instantly killing Bloody Knife, the latter mounted at Major Reno's side. It was alleged that the explosiveness of this incident unnerved Reno to a considerable extent. Utley, *The Reno Court of Inquiry: The Chicago Times Account,* pp. 255-57.

[6] Red Feather's account is not quite clear about the location where this flagbearer was shot. We know that Sergeant Myles F. O'Hara of M Company was shot on the skirmish line outside the woods. O'Hara was abandoned by Edward D. Pigford who ignored his Sergeant's pleas for help and hastily retreated. Maybe Red Feather made reference to O'Hara, although it seems unlikely that a first sergeant would have been encumbered with guidon duties. It should be noted further that military dignitaries were shown in later years a location on Reno's skirmish line where the first soldier was slain. According to the Indian informants, who now had enlisted as Indian Scouts, this soldier had worn a "large yellow stipe down the side of his trousers," suggesting the identity of an NCO. Further examination of this location revealed a remnant of a trousers' leg on which the yellow stripe was still discernable, further proof that this was the location where O'Hara was slain; see Miles, *Personal Recollections,* p. 287; Col. Homer W. Wheeler, *Buffalo Days* (Indianapolis, 1925), p. 179.

[7] Red Feather's statement about these soldiers may have reference to several troopers who fled up the valley. One of these escaped in the timber below the mouth of Reno Creek. However, two others were less fortunate because they were overtaken and killed a short distance up the valley by pursuing Sioux and Cheyennes; see Marquis, *Wooden Leg,* pp. 222-23.

late in getting to the camp. He came amongst the soldiers.[8]

The soldiers all had six shooters in their hands and held off the Indians for a while. Red Feather could not get close, but shot as many horses from under the soldiers as he could. Red Feather saw a soldier fall off his horse, his foot caught in the stirrup, and he was dragged through the creek. A Ree was killed by the Oglalas near the river, the Standing Rock Indians recognizing [him] as probably being a scout.[9]

Below the point the soldiers crossed, they saw two men in white shirts and blue trousers running across the river; afterwards found they were scouts. Kicking Bear took after them and shouted, "These two are Indians—Palani[!]" Red Feather shot the horse from under one and Kicking Bear followed the other and shot the first one twice.[10] Red Feather stabbed him to death.

The Indians followed the soldiers; ten of them got upon a hill.[11] About ten o'clock the soldiers made a defense. The women and children shouted, "Another detachment

[8]Crazy Horse's delay was attributed to his lengthy incantations to invoke the spiritual powers for both himself and his pony. Apparently, these rites took so much time that the young men of his soldiers' lodge could hardly restrain their impatience. Crazy Horse was one of the few Indian leaders who were able to exercise some measure of authority over fellow tribesmen.

[9]The sequence in the narration of events suggests that the Ree killed near the river was Bloody Knife, who was half Hunkpapa Lakota.

[10]Born in an Oglala camp in 1848, Kicking Bear grew up to become a crafty warrior and a close ally of Crazy Horse, to whom he may have been related. He married a niece of the Minneconjou, Big Foot, and he later became a minor chief in that band. His main rise to notoriety came through his leading part in the Ghost Dance troubles of 1890. The Sioux word *Palani* was used to identify members of an enemy tribe, specifically the Pawnees and "Arickarees." In this instance, *Palani* meant Ree Indian. Fearing reprisals by the whites for the killing and mutilation of Uncle Sam's soldiers, the Indians showed a reluctance to relate their involvement in these slayings. However, no such restraint was exhibited when narrating the killings of the Rees. Although only three Rees were killed in total—Bloody Knife, Bobtail Bull and Little Brave—the number of their slayers and coup counters has swollen steadily over the years.

[11]The battle strength of Reno's combat force consisted of 11 officers, 129 elistees, 4 civilians, and 31 Indian Scouts, for a total of 175 men. The casualties sustained during

coming!'' They were on the high place. There was another body of soldiers east of the Cheyennes. They left Reno and went as fast as possible to the other end, but the Cheyennes were already fighting. The Oglalas acted as reinforcements.

The Indians charged twice in the battle at the lower end of the camp. The first time the [Custer] soldiers were on foot. Then they retreated to their horses. In the first charge, Red Feather's horse was shot from under him.[12] He came to an officer who was shot through the stomach who was sitting on the ground, holding a gun in his hand. Red Feather tried to take the gun away, but the officer dropped the gun and grabbed Red Feather. Red Feather was scared to death until someone shot the officer. The cartridges stuck in the [officer's] gun because it was too smoked from shooting.[13]

When the soldiers got to their horses, they retreated. There was a deep place in the timber that was a good place for defense, but instead they took to the open country which made it easier for the Indians to catch them. The

---

the valley fight and the subsequent retreat to Reno Hill amounted to 3 officers, 32 enlistees, 2 civilians, and 3 Indian scouts, for a dead count of 40 men. We may deduce, therefore, that some 135 men of Reno's combat force eventually gained the safety of the bluffs, which is far more than the 10 spoken of by Red Feather. For an excellent statistical study of the battle strength, see Gray, *Centennial Campaign,* pp. 284-97.

[12]The action mentioned here has reference to the fighting around Calhoun Hill because the narrative goes on to state that the soldiers should have moved instead into the sheltering timber along the river. The open country of Calhoun Hill sealed their defeat.

[13]Although some carbines may have malfunctioned due to faulty extractor mechanisms, a recent artifact study discloses that the extractor failure amounted to less than 0.35 percent of some 1,751 tested 45/55 casings. It should be quite obvious, therefore, that this problem was not a determining factor in the outcome of the battle. See Paul L. Hedren, ''Carbine Extraction Failure at the Little Big Horn: A New Examination,'' *Military Collector and Historian* (Summer, 1973): 66-68; Douglass D. Scott and Richard A. Fox, Jr., *Archaeological Insights into the Custer Battle* (Norman, 1987), p. 81.

U.S. Military rank identifications by the Indians should be viewed with some skepticism. Their (mis)conception of rank insignia, especially of military personnel in the field, may have been subject to confusion of noncommissioned officers with commissioned ones.

Indians in the lead were the younger men, [who] didn't have enough experience and were reckless. The older ones held off for safety. The younger men were killed mostly, and they [the young men] took most of the guns. When the soldiers reached their horses, they were met by the Indians coming from the side; the soldiers took to a slant.[14]

One soldier on a sorrel horse tried to get around the Indians. He was on a sorrel horse with white legs. The Indians took after him, and shot and shot at him, but couldn't hit him or catch him. They saw some smoke and the report of a gun, and saw him fall off his horse. The Indians went over and [concluded] he had shot himself. Someone of the Uncpapa band got the horse and tied him to a stake. Everyone went to look at it. Gen. Scott: "I had information that the soldier, while using his revolver as a quirt, accidently shot himself." Red Feather: "All the soldiers were drunk. They didn't know what they were doing."[15]

---

[14]The sequence of subsequent events suggests that this action took place east of Custer Ridge and involved I Company. Some of these reckless young men may have been referred to by John Stands in Timber when he spoke of young boys taking the suicide vows "to throw their lives away fighting." Stands in Timber and Liberty, *Cheyenne Memories*, p. 194.

[15]Red Feather's answer is symbolic in expression in that it means to convey that the troopers *acted* as though drunk. Erratic behavior based on fear resulted in the uncharacteristic lack of military discipline in Custer's troopers, which strange behavior was duly noted by their Indian adversaries. The question of drunkenness was initially raised by two Cheyennes, Two Moons and Wooden Leg, whose statements were later discredited through the investigatory efforts of John Stands in Timber and Dr. Thomas B. Marquis. The latter, who gave this matter his special attention, concluded that whiskey did not influence the conduct of the soldiers that day, and that this whole matter had too thin a basis to be given serious consideration. See *Billings* (Montana) *Gazette*, 5/27/1961; Marquis, *Wooden Leg*, pp. 246, 248; Stands in Timber and Liberty, *Cheyenne Memories*, p. 205; Marquis, *Keep the Last Bullet for Yourself* (New York City, 1976), p. 129.

Perhaps the Lakotas later provided the best explanation of the strange behavior of Custer's soldiers. The Hunkpapa, Shoots Walking, recalled that the soldiers acted as though they were drunk; that they did not seem to know how to shoot; that many of them threw their guns down; and that they fought without any system whatsoever. This opinion was shared by Red Horse, a Minneconjou, who stated that Custer's soldiers became

The soldiers halted and dismounted and got on a hill; the Indians dismounted, too, and followed on hands and knees. They couldn't get near, but some crept up. When the soldiers left their horses, the Indians picked them up. The Indians sneaked up the hill in the ravine and [took cover] behind sagebrush. Red Feather's horse had been shot under him, so he was with the others who were on foot. If either side showed a head, the other side would shoot him down. An old man, Flying By, who wore a shirt and had his hair tied behind his head, kept shouting, which encouraged the young men. He was the only old man in front with the young ones. Arrows were a great deal used. The soldiers were without caps now.[16]

The Indians hid behind little rolls. The soldiers were on one side of the hill and the Indians on the other, a slight rise between them. While they were lying there shooting at one another, Crazy Horse came up on horseback—with an

foolish, and that many threw away their guns and raised their hands in a sign of surrender. Bear Lying Down, an Oglala, remembered that Custer's troopers fired wildly into the air and acted as if intoxicated, which agrees with the statement of his tribesman, He Dog, who distinctly recalled that some of the soldiers feigned death by playing possum, but that none were drunk. Two Bulls, a Yanktonai Nakota, compared the behavior of Custer's troopers with that of boys, while Standing Bear, the father of Luther, found very little honor in combatting such frightened adversaries. See Walter Campbell Collection, Univeristy of Oklahoma, box 111; Graham, *The Custer Myth,* p. 62; Walter Camp Manuscripts, Indiana University Library, p. 269; Edward A. Milligan, *High Noon on the Greasy Grass* (Bottineau, 1972), no pagination; Luther Standing Bear, *My People the Sioux* (Lincoln, 1975), p. 83. Reviewing this evidence, there exists little doubt that the strange behavior displayed by Custer's troopers was *not* the result of alcohol consumption, but rather it was caused by fear, which ultimately led to panic.

[16]The Flying By mentioned in the narrative was an elderly Oglala Lakota. He should not be confused with his Minneconjou namesake, the son of Lame Deer, who was born in 1850, and who was in the prime of his life when the Custer battle took place.

[17]The extent of Crazy Horse's participation in the Custer battle is only just now becoming clear. Red Feather's narrative reveals that Crazy Horse had made a bravery run in front of Custer's soldiers. This display of valorous contempt for the marksmanship of the whites left a lasting impression on the Arapaho, Waterman, who vividly recalled that the Oglala Chief was the bravest man he ever saw, and that he rode closest to the soldiers, yelling back encouragements to his warriors. Awed by such valor, Waterman noted that all the soldiers were shooting at Crazy Horse, but that none was able to hit him.

eagle horn—and rode between the two parties. The soldiers all fired at once, but didn't hit him. The Indians got the idea the soldiers' guns were empty and charged immediately on the soldiers. They charged right over the hill. Red Feather, yelling, shot into the soldiers who tried to get away. That made it easier for the Indians, who shot them from behind.[17]

Red Feather didn't follow them very far, but interested himself in taking saddlebags. He got four, with ground coffee and ammunition in them. Also a little can with something in it. He tasted it, and it was whiskey. It was a terrible battle. The worst he had ever seen, and he, Red Feather, has had some experience. Red Feather considered it a hard battle because both sides were brave warriors.

This action occurred on the east side of Custer Ridge near Keogh's location, because it was here that Crazy Horse later charged and broke through a gap, splitting Custer's troopers into two bunches. This charge resulted in the annihilation of Keogh's company and caused many grey horses to break away from Custer Ridge, leaving E Company afoot. There exists sufficient evidence to suggest that this led to the flight of some forty troopers later on, nearly all of whom were slain in Deep Ravine.

These bravery runs were generally made for the greater glorification of the rider. However, in this instance the purpose was to draw and waste the enemy's fire. Having thus emptied the soldiers' single-shot carbines, the Indians would swiftly charge on their adversaries with minimal risk to themselves. This was a tried and proven method which was fully mastered by the Plains Indians. Such strategy was indeed intended in the Custer Fight because the Hunkpapa, Shoots Walking, made clear that a number of young men, some without firearms, charged into the soldiers immediately after drawing their fire.

In later years, the Minneconjou, Lazy White Bull, tried to minimize the battle feats of Crazy Horse. However, the latter was highly revered among the Lakotas who spoke of this favored Oglala son as "Our Brave Man." His charisma was well remembered by He Dog who fondly recalled in old age that everybody became brave when Crazy Horse appeared on the battlefield. The Oglala, Foolish Elk, shared the same sentiment, stating that Crazy Horse was the greatest leader and warrior in the Custer Battle. And these laudatory statements were also spoken by the Cheyennes, who commented further that "Crazy Horse had the nerve," meaning, they said, he was the bravest of all in the battle. See Graham, *The Custer Myth*, p. 110; Charles E. De Land, *The Sioux Wars*, South Dakota Historical *Collections*, Vol. XV (1930), p. 721; Hammer, *Custer in '76* p. 207; Vestal, *Warpath*, pp. 196-97; Joseph G. Masters, *Shadows Fall Across the Little Horn* (Laramie, 1951), pp. 41n., 50n.

THE HUNKPAPA LAKOTA, MOVING ROBE WOMAN
This picture was taken by F.B. Fiske of Fort Yates, North Dakota,
ca. 1937, when Moving Robe Woman was about 83 years old.
Courtesy of National Anthropological Archives, Smithsonian Institution.

The Moving Robe Woman Interview

Editorial note: This interview was conducted in 1931 by Frank B. Zahn and was eventually published in the columns of the Pinedale Roundup. *The article contains a lengthy introduction by the newspaper editor, which I have omitted. The following transcript of the newspaper clipping includes only the statements attributed to Moving Robe.*

Moving Robe Woman
Standing Rock Agency
North Dakota
[1931][1]

I was born seventy-seven winters ago, near Grand River, South Dakota. My father, Slohan [Crawler], was the bravest man among our people. Fifty-five years ago, we packed our tents and went with other Indians to Peji Sla Wakapa

---

[1] Born about 1854, Moving Robe Woman was the daughter of the Hunkpapa Lakota, Crawler, a celebrated warrior who was instrumental in the release of Fanny Kelly from Sioux captivity in 1864. On the Standing Rock Agency rolls, Moving Robe is listed under her father's name, and having been given a Christian first name, she became known to the whites as Mary Crawler. Moving Robe's account of the Custer Battle appeared originally in the *St. Paul Pioneer Press*. It was reprinted in the *Pinedale* (Wyoming) *Roundup*, of which an undated clipping is filed with the Agnes W. Spring Collection, University of Wyoming Heritage Center, Laramie. Moving Robe's recollections were obtained through the services of Frank B. Zahn (1891-1966), who was an agency interpreter and later the

(Greasy Grass [Little Bighorn]).[2] We were then living on
the Standing Rock reservation. I belonged to Sitting Bull's
band. They were great fighters. We called ourselves
Hunkpapa. This means confederate bands.[3] When I was
still a young girl (about 17) I accompanied a Sioux war
party which made war against the Crow Indians in
Montana.

I am going to tell you of the greatest battle. This was a
fight against Pehin Hanska (General Custer).[4] I was several
miles from the Hunkpapa camp when I [saw a] cloud of
dust rise beyond a ridge of bluffs in the east. The morning
was hot and sultry. Several of us Indian girls were digging
wild turnips. I was then 23 years old. We girls looked
towards camp and saw a warrior ride swiftly, shouting that
the soldiers were only a few miles away, and that the women
and children, including old men, should run for the hills in
an opposite direction.

I dropped the pointed ash stick which I had used in
digging turnips, and ran towards my tipi (teepee). I saw my
father running towards the horses. When I got to my tent,
mother told me that news was brought to her that my

---

presiding judge of the Standing Rock Court of Indian Offenses. It is interesting to note
that Judge Zahn was the son of Flying Hawk's daughter and William P. Zahn, a former
soldier who had served in the 17th U.S. Infantry at Custer's Fort Lincoln. See Vestal,
Sitting Bull, Champion of the Sioux, pp. 64, 66; *Bismark Tribune,* 7/5/1966.

[2] The stream called Greasy Grass by the Sioux was identified by the Cheyennes as Goat
River, and by the Crows as Little Big Horn. Since it was named after the mountain sheep
which dwell in this region, the English name for the river should be written as "Little
Bighorn." See Hammer, *Custer in '76,* pp. 161, 212; Walter Camp Manuscripts, Indiana
University Library, p. 824.

[3] Although the Sioux word *Lakota* means "confederate bands," the word *Hunkpapa*
properly translates into People Who Camp at the Entrance," meaning the eastern
entrance in a circle of lodges. See Hassrick, *The Sioux,* pp. 3, 13; McLaughlin, *My Friend
the Indian,* p. 7.

[4] *Pehin Hanska,* literally translated as "Hair Long", was the Lakota name for Gen.
George A. Custer. Although this name was also adopted by the Northern Cheyennes, the
southern branch referred to Custer as Red Nose, which name resulted from the extreme
sunburns Custer received during the field campaigns on the Southern Plains. Walter
Camp Manuscripts, Indiana University Library, p. 21.

brother had been killed by the soldiers. In a few moments we saw soldiers on horseback on a bluff just across the Greasy Grass River.[5]

I heard Hawk Man shout, "Hoka He! Hoka He! (Charge! Charge!)".[6] The soldiers began firing into our camp. Then they ceased firing. I saw my father preparing to go to the battle. I sang a death song for my brother who had been killed. My heart was bad. Revenge! Revenge! For my brother's death. I thought of the death of my young brother, One Hawk.[7] I ran to a nearby thicket and got my black horse. I painted my face with crimson and braided my black hair. I was mourning. I was a woman, but I was not afraid.

By this time, the soldiers (Reno's men) were forming a battle line in the bottom about a half mile away. In another moment, I heard a terrific volley of carbines. The bullets shattered the tipi poles. Women and children were running away from the gunfire. In the tumult I heard old men and women singing death songs for their warriors who were now ready to attack the soldiers. The enchanting death songs made me brave, although I was a woman. I saw a warrior adjusting his quiver and grasping his tomahawk. He started running towards his horse, when he suddenly recoiled and dropped dead. He was killed near his tipi.

---

[5] There are other Lakotas who confirm this statement. After many years of diligent inquiries, Indian Agent James McLaughlin learned that the southern camps were alerted by the unexpected sight of soldiers on the bluffs, and that Reno's sudden appearance in the valley came as a complete surprise to these startled Indians. See the statements by Gall and Pretty White Buffalo Woman to James McLaughlin in *My Friend the Indian*, pp. 36, 38, 44. However, it is quite certain that Custer's descent of Reno Creek had been sighted earlier by Indians collected near Reno Hill, and that these men signalled Custer's approach by waving their saddle blankets to the camps below. See Hammer, *Custer in '76* p. 92 n3, n6.

[6] Hawk Man was a Hunkpapa head soldier who was killed by a gunshot in front of Reno's skirmish line in the valley.

[7] One Hawk, or Lone Hawk, may have been the formal name of the boy generally known as Deeds.

Warriors were given orders by Hawk Man to mount their horses and follow the fringe of the forest and wait until commands were given to charge. The soldiers kept firing. Some women were also killed.[8] Father led my black horse up to me and I mounted. We galloped towards the soldiers. Other warriors joined in with us. When we were nearing the fringe of the woods, an order was given by Hawk Man to charge. The warriors were now near the soldiers. The troopers were all on foot. They shot straight, because I saw our leader killed as he rode with his warriors.

The charge was so stubborn that the soldiers ran to their horses and, mounting them, rode swiftly towards the river. Their horses had to swim to get across. Some of the warriors rode into the water and tomahawked the soldiers. In the charge, the Indians rode among the troopers and with tomahawks unhorsed several of them. The Indians chased the soldiers across the river and up over a bluff.

Then the warriors returned to the bottom where the first battle took place. The warriors rode in a column of fives. They sang a victory song. Someone said that another body of soldiers was attacking the lower end of the village. I heard afterwards that these soldiers were under the command of Long Hair (Custer). With my father and other youthful warriors I rode in that direction.[9]

---

[8] This statement is corroborated by the *Bismarck Tribune* of 7/6/1876, which reveals that ten women had been killed, alleged to have been the work of Reno's Indian auxiliaries. Among the slain was probably the family of the Hunkpapa, Gall.

[9] Moving Robe's participation in the Custer Battle is corroborated by the Hunkpapa, Rain in the Face, who near the end of his life still recalled his reaction upon seeing her: "'Behold, there is among us a young woman!' I shouted. 'Let no young man hide behind her garment!' I knew that would make these young men brave! The woman was Tashenamani [Tashna Mani], or Moving Robe, whose brother had just been killed. Holding her brother's war staff over her head, and leaning forward upon her charger, she looked as pretty as a bird." See Eastman, "Rain-in-the-Face," p. 511. Although reticent to tell Zahn the details of her involvement, it was learned, nonetheless, that Moving Robe fought Custer's troopers as fiercely as any of the warriors. She had secured a revolver, and when the battle was over she had killed two of Custer's wounded troopers—shooting one,

We crossed the Greasy Grass below a beaver dam (the water is not so deep there) and came upon many horses. One soldier was holding the reins of eight or ten horses.[10] An Indian waved his blanket and scared all the horses. They got away from the men (troopers). On the ridge just north of us, I saw blueclad men running up a ravine, firing as they ran. The valley was dense with powder smoke. I never heard such whooping and shouting. "There is never a better time to die!" shouted Red Horse.[11]

Long Hair's troopers were trapped in an enclosure. There were Indians everywhere. The Cheyennes attacked the soldiers from the north, and Crow King from the south.[12] It was not a massacre, but a hotly contested battle between two armed forces. Very few soldiers were muti-lated, as oft has been said by the whites. Not a single soldier was burned at the stake. Sioux Indians do not torture their victims.[13]

After the battle the Indians took all the equipment and horses belonging to the soldiers. The brave men who came to punish us that morning were defeated; but in the end the

and hacking the other man to death with her sheath knife. See Nelly Snyder Yost, *Boss Cowman: The Recollections of Ed Lemmon, 1857-1946* (Lincoln, 1969), p. 88.

[10]Cavalry companies were divided in sets of fours, and when ordered to dismount and fight on foot, the horses of each set were held by one trooper, freeing the other three to concentrate on combat activities. Considering the stresses caused by combat noise, it would have been virtually impossible for one man to control four horses by merely holding them by their reins. For that reason, the bridle was supplied with a strap on each side, along with a snap ring, which allowed the holder to link the bridles of the four horses together. See Magnussen, *Peter Thompson's Narrative*, p. 117, n19. When Moving Robe saw these horseholders near Calhoun Hill, she noticed them burdened with twice the number normally allowed, which suggest a heightening crisis in which horseholders were deployed on the front line.

[11]Red Horse was a respected tribal chief of the Minneconjou Lakotas whose band surrendered at Cheyenne River Agency in 1877. For his two accounts of the Custer Battle, see Graham, *The Custer Myth*, pp. 56-62.

[12]Crow King was a Hunkpapa Lakota who gained prominence after his surrender to the U.S. Military in 1880. His progressive leadership is noted in McLaughlin, *My Friend the Indian*, pp. 21-25. For Crow's King's account of the Custer Battle, see Judson Elliott Walker, *The Campaigns of General Custer* (New York, 1966), pp. 101-103.

Indians lost. We saw the body of Long Hair. Of course, we did not know who the soldiers were until an interpreter told us that the men came from Ft. Lincoln, then Dakota Territory. On the saddle blankets were the crossed saber insignia and the figure "7".

Over sixty Indians were killed, and they were brought back to the camp for scaffold burial. The Indians did not stage a victory dance that night. They were mourning for their own dead.

The next day we packed our tents and started north to the Canadian line. We crossed the border and remained in Canada for four years. We were brought down by steamboats in the spring of 1881. Sitting Bull surrendered to the military at Ft. Buford. In his death, the Sioux Nation lost a great leader. They are all dead now—Sitting Bull, Rain in the Face, Crow King, Gall, Crazy Horse, Red Cloud, Flying Cloud, and soon the Great Spirit will call the remaining warriors.

In this narrative, I have not boasted of my conquests. I am a woman, but I fought for my people. The white man will never understand the Indian. Eyas Hen La! I have said everything!

---

[13] Moving Robe is contradicted by not only the Cheyenne, Two Moons, but also by her Hunkpapa tribesman, Little Knife, who admitted in 1879, that a soldier with stripes on his arm (NCO) had been taken prisoner and was killed during a wild dance held later that night. *Billings* (Montana) *Gazette*, partially dated, 1926, clipping in Billings Clipping File, Billings Public Library. On the subject of captives, Sergeant John M. Ryan recalled: "I think the Indians took some of our men prisoners, and when the reinforcements joined us, we found what appeared to be human bones and parts of blue uniforms where the men had been tied to stakes and trees. . . . We found three of our men's heads, suspended by wires through the back of the ears from a lodge pole, with the hair burned off." *Hardin* (Montana) *Tribune*, 6/22/1923. Unable to forget the horrors of the Little Bighorn, Major Reno wrote: "Many of their skulls had been crushed in; eyes had been torn from their sockets; hands, feet, arms, legs and noses had been wrenched off; many had their flesh cut in stips the entire length of their bodies, and there were others whose limbs were closely perforated with bullet holes, showing that the torture had been inflicted while the wretched victims were yet alive." See Hardorff, *The Custer Battle Casualties*, pp. 97-98.

THE OGLALA LAKOTA, EAGLE ELK
This picture was taken by John G. Neihardt in 1944,
when Eagle Elk was about 93 years old.
Photo courtesy of Hilda Neihardt Petri and John G. Neihardt Trust.

The Eagle Elk Interview

Editorial note; This interview was conducted in 1944 by John G. Neihardt. The interview resulted in 49 double-spaced pages of typescript by Neihardt's daughter, the present Hilda Neihardt Petri. Only three manuscript pages are in reference to the Custer Battle, of which the following is a verbatim transcript.

Eagle Elk
Pine Ridge Agency
November 27, 1944[1]

Different bands were camped [together]. They had a victory dance all night. Next morning I came towards this camp. There was a battle on a creek called Rosebud. Some

[1] The son of Long Whirlwind and Pretty Feather Woman, the Oglala named Eagle Elk was born in the fall of 1851, near the confluence of the White and Missouri rivers. Although born of a Yankton Nakota mother, he grew up among his father's people, the *Oyukhpe* Oglalas (People Who Lay Down Their Packs), a powerful band of the Smoke People (Northern Oglalas) who moved into the Powder River region in the late 1850s. Eagle Elk was a member of the *Hoksi Hakakta*, or Last Child Society, an unusual military lodge whose forty members consisted of the last born males of selected families. Under the leadership of Eagle Elk's older cousin, the renowned Crazy Horse, this lodge achieved a reputation of fearlessness, many of its young men serving as his bodyguard. In addition to the customary confrontations with enemy tribes, Eagle Elk participated in many of the fights with the whites, among which the Fetterman Battle of 1866, and the Custer Battle a

of them came back and had a victory dance. About four days later the Custer fight took place.[2] When day came, it must have been about eight in the morning, when the people stopped dancing to eat.[3] Just at that time, a Hunkpapa woman called me and said, "Attackers are approaching fast, they say." (Natan uskay.) While I was with the others, a second call from the same woman repeated the same thing: "Natan uskay." I said, "I am going home. There is something to that [warning]." Someone said, "Don't go. They are not going to kill us all at once."

I took my blanket and started [walking] and someone came along and said, "Friend, I am going home, too." It was Red Feather.[4] We started together across the camp circle. Just then we heard shooting towards the river. Red Feather and I ran and got to our home. Just at this moment my brother had driven the ponies in from the water. As we were running to our teepee, I came across a pony that I

---

decade later. In 1871, Eagle Elk married a Sans Arc woman, and after the surrender of the Sioux, his family settled down in the Wounded Knee District on Pine Ridge Agency. Some sixty years later, from November 27 through December 1, 1944, Eagle Elk granted an interview to Dr. John G. Neihardt. This interview was recorded by Neihardt's daugher, Hilda, whose transcript totals some 49 pages. It is of interest to note that this material became the basis for Dr. Neihardt's work, *When the Tree Flowered: An Authentic Tale of the Old Sioux World* (New York, 1951), in which its fictionalized narrator, Eagle Voice, told of his life. The Eagle Elk manuscript is contained in the John G. Neihardt Collection, Joint Collection University of Missouri Library and State Historical Society of Missouri, Columbia. The material dealing with the Custer Battle is here reproduced by special permission from the John G. Neihardt Trust.

[2]The Rosebud Battle occurred on Saturday, June 17, 1876, while the Custer Battle took place eight days later, on Sunday, June 25. It is not quite clear when this victory dance was held. However, since the Indians had sustained a number of casualties, it seems probable that the celebration did not take place until June 21, after the customary four days of mourning had been observed.

[3]These dances were held all over the great village on the evening of June 24, but the Cheyenne, Wooden Leg, identifies the celebrations as a "social affair for young people [and] not a ceremonial or war dance." Marquis, *Wooden Leg*, pp. 215-16.

[4]This individual was probably the Oglala, Red Feather, whose 1920 interview with Gen. Hugh L. Scott is given heretofore. On the evening of Saturday, June 24, Red Feather had remained up very late because "he had been dancing and was after the girls."

knew belonged to a relative, so I caught the pony and rode him. I then got my own horse and gun. I was on a fresh horse and started towards where the excitement was going on.

I went a little way and another Indian came along, and he had a horse that belonged to me and was a good horse. I changed to that horse and went right on. Just about that time they were chasing the soldiers. The older people ran away, but the Indian men went right out to fight the soldiers on foot. As I was going along, I saw that the Indians were chasing the soldiers. There were two Indians, one on a black and the other on a white horse, chasing the soldiers. Suddenly, the man on the white horse got among the soldiers. He had a sword and used it to kill one soldier. The other Indian fell off his horse.[5] The horse ran back to the camp. Some man brought the horse back, and that man was Crazy Horse. I did not see where Crazy Horse went from there.

As I was going along, my brother came, and he had a gun, too. He wanted my gun, which was a Winchester; and so I gave it to him and took his. As I went along, I saw a man sitting on the ground, and a woman came along and stopped by him, and first I thought she was pointing at him. She drew back her arm and pointed at him again, and the gun [she was holding] went off and the man dropped. The man was a Hunkpapa who was with the soldiers, and [he] got wounded and fell off his horse.[6] When the woman came up, he said that her husband, or son, must [have] be[en] shot in the battle. She came with her gun, and the man said, "Do not kill me, because I will be dead in a short while, anyway."

---

[5]The Custer Battle pictographs of the Oglala, Amos Bad Heart Bull, contain five drawings of warriors armed with sabers, of which three pictographs depict the act of killing Reno's troopers. See Blish, *A Pictographic History of the Oglala Sioux*, pp. 228, 234, 341, 243, and 250.

The woman said, "If you did not want to be killed, why did you not stay home where you belong and not come to attack us?" The first time she pointed the gun it did not go off, but the second time it killed him. I heard that this woman is still living among the Hunkpapas. Her name is Her Eagle Robe (Tashina Wamnbli).[7]

Then I saw that a bunch of Indians were chasing the soldiers up the creek. It was deep and flooded. The Indians could kill the soldiers in the water as they tried to swim [across]. There were two men who ran away from the rest up the hill. They were two Rees who were with the soldiers. They were singing as they ran away, so we knew they were Indians.[8] I was not doing very much, but was keeping back

[6]The individual slain by this Lakota woman was Isaiah Dorman, a Negro interpreter employed at Fort Rice, located near the border of present North and South Dakota. In the early 1870s he maintained a woodyard just north of Fort Yates where he and his Hunkpapa wife lived in a dugout, its shallow excavation still visible in the 1930s. He accompanied the expedition as a civilian interpreter for Custer's five Sioux Indian Scouts. During Reno's retreat from the valley floor, Dorman was recognized and singled out after killing a hostile at close range. Known among the Lakotas as Teat, his horse was riddled with bullets and fell over on its back, sealing Dorman's fate. See Dixon, *The Vanishing Race*, p. 173; Vestal, *Sitting Bull, Champion of the Sioux*, pp. 165-66; Frank Zahn memorandum, undated, Walter S. Campbell Collection, University of Oklahoma Library, Box 104, item #4. For an excellent, capsule biography of Dorman, see William Boyes, *Custer's Black White Man (Washington, 1972)*.

[7]After the battle, Dorman's body was found amidst a prairie dog town, about a hundred yards southeast of the stretch of timber which sheltered Reno's skirmish line. His remains bore the signs of extreme mutilation, the result of hatred shown to kindred judged to be traitors to their own kind. The skin of his legs from the knees down bore the holes caused by small pistol balls, an inch or two apart. His stomach was slashed open and the blood drained into a coffee pot and cup which Dorman carried on his person. His breast was riddled with arrows, and an iron picket pin was driven through his testicles, pinning him to the ground. His penis was cut off and stuffed into his mouth, an act regarded among the Sioux as the worst possible insult. Dorman was judged by his contemporaries as a man of considerable intelligence, one who enjoyed the respect and confidence from all who knew him, both red and white alike. It comes as no surprise, therefore, that Eagle Elk vividly recalled the details of this gruesome incident, even after some seventy years. See Libby, *The Arikara Narrative*, p. 110; Hammer, Custer in '76, pp. 223-24; Camp Manuscripts, Indiana University Library, p. 676; Camp Notes, Brigham Young University Library, p. 258.

and watching. The two [Ree] Indians escaped and ran up the hill. Before they got away, a Sioux rode up to them and was going to attack the Ree. The Ree shot the Sioux, and he fell off his horse. After that a man with long hair and all stripped got right up to him and they were both on the ground, and the Ree and Sioux were shooting at each other. The Ree was shot down and fell.[9] Just at that time, the other Ree was fighting with another Sioux, and the Ree shot the Sioux off his horse.[10] The stripped man shot the Ree.

I did not see any soldiers who escaped; all I saw were killed. Just about that time, some Indians started a fire because soldiers were hiding in the tall grass.[11] Just then someone said more soldiers [Custer's battalion] were

---

[8]This was probably a military lodge song which words encouraged the Ree singer and his companion to be brave.

[9]Custer's auxiliary force of Rees numbered some 25 warriors, of which three were slain with Reno's command in the valley. Their names were Bloody Knife, Bobtail Bull, and Little Brave. The Ree mentioned here was probably Little Brave who sustained a gunshot wound in the right shoulder during the valley retreat. He had taken shelter on a little elevation near the river and killed one of his adversaries, the Sans Arc, Elk Stands Above. After a short fire exchange, Little Brave's position was overrun and he was beaten and stabbed to death by Wooden Leg and others. Identification of his remains was made impossible due to a crushed skull. See Libby, *The Arikara Narrative,* p. 126; Blish, *A Pictographic History of the Oglala Sioux,* p. 247, which contains a pictograph depicting this incident; Marquis, *Wooden Leg,* p. 224.

[10]The identity of the second Ree was Bobtail Bull, leader of the Arikara force, who had charged and killed the Cheyenne, Whirlwind, east of the river near Reno's retreat crossing. Eagle Elk mistakenly identified Whirlwind as a Sioux. Bobtail Bull was subsequently slain by the Oglala, Running Eagle. See Marquis, *Wooden Leg,* p. 224; Blish, *A Pictographic History of the Oglala Sioux,* p. 246, which pictograph probably depicts this incident. For a modern study of Custer's Ree Indian Scouts, see John S. Gray, "Arikara Scouts with Custer," *North Dakota History* (Spring, 1968): 444-78.

[11]As a result of Major Reno's disorganized withdrawal from the woods, some 20 troopers and civilians were left behind. One of these was the interpreter, Fred F. Gerard, who recalled that "after the troops had withdrawn, the Indians set fire to the timber, and it was burning close to where we were sitting. The smoke was very dense." Utley, *The Reno Court of Inquiry: The Chicago Times Account,* p. 96. Eventually, all of these individuals reached the safety of Reno Hill, except two soldiers who had cached considerable amounts of money in the woods and who refused to come out. See Hammer, *Custer in '76,* p. 224.

coming. There was a party of eight Indians and I who started that way and got to a point where they could see there were soldiers all right. We nine went down and saw the [Custer] soldiers on the ridge. Before we crossed the water, we were the first to make a charge. One man went out of the bunch and took away the flag that one soldier had. The Cheyenne was shot through the heels, and his horse stumbled and broke his legs.[12] We went right up to the soldiers. Just at this moment we noticed that the other Indians were charging from the south end.[13] From that time, the others were coming across the creek after the soldiers. The soldiers were shooting a lot, so the Indians were thrown back.

I saw a yellow spotted horse running and no man was on him. Just then I saw an Indian running who was shot through the jaw, and [he] was all bloody.[14] My brother saw him and came up and helped him, and then we went on chasing the soldiers. I had a brother with me, and as we

[12]This may have been the Cheyenne, Yellow Nose; however, there were several brave men among the Sioux who performed similar feats. One of these was the Oglala, Stands First, who captured Custer's personal flag. See Marquis, *Wooden Leg*, p. 266; Edward S. Curtis, *The North American Indian*, Vol. III (Cambridge, 1908). p. 189. For an excellent article on the Seventh's guidons, headquarters flag, and the regimental standard, see William A. Graham, "Custer's Battle Flags," *The* (Los Angeles) *Westerners Brand Book, 1950* (Los Angeles, 1951): 121-34.

[13]Eagle Elk's party charged the west end of Calhoun Ridge, also known as Greasy Grass Hill. For corroboration of the action at this location, see the account by the Cheyenne, White Shield, in Grinnell, *The Fighting Cheyennes* pp. 350-51.

[14]The plight of this wounded man was commented on by several other eyewitnesses. The Minneconjou Lakota, Standing Bear, told Dr. Neihardt that he was on the west side of Custer Ridge when he saw this "Sioux with blood in his mouth. He was very dizzy. He stood up and then began to come down again." DeMallie, *The Sixth Grandfather*, p. 185. A similar observation was made by the Cheyenne, Wooden Leg, who, however, reported seeing this man while east of Custer Ridge. "I saw one Sioux walking slowly toward the gulch, going away from where were the soldiers. He wabbled dizzily as he moved along. He fell down, got up, fell down again, got up again. As he passed near to where I was I saw that his whole lower jaw was shot away. The sight of him made me sick. I had to vomit. "Marquis, *Wooden Leg*, p. 234.

made a charge, they shot back very heavily, so we swung back. Just then my brother's horse was running [off] and he was not on him. I thought he was shot off, and just at that moment there were four soldiers' horses running.[15] I chased after them. I was chasing the horses and got two of them, and gave them to another Indian. At that moment I saw a horse shot through the head near the ear. He did not drop, but went around and around [in a circle].

An Indian came and said, "Your cousin is shot off his horse. He is lying over there." But I did not go back to look for him. Another man said, "There is a man shot through the head." I found him and saw the man. He wore a bird on his head, and the bullet went through the bird and his head. One of the soldiers' horses that I caught (above) was bay and the other sorrel.[16] The bridle reins were tied together. I got off my horse and another man was getting off. This man who was shot through—we went there; and it was behind a ridge so there was no danger.

[15] Cavalry horses were held in sets of four, and the fact that such a set was runnning loose may indicate that the designated horseholder had become incapacitated. Of this particular set, Eagle Elk caught two and found the bridles linked together, probably by means of the special snap ring.

[16] In the fall of 1868, the horses of the Seventh Cavalry were classified and arranged throughout the companies according to color. In reference to Custer's battalion at the Little Bighorn, this rearrangement had led to the following distribution: Companies F, I and L had bay horses; Company C had light sorrels, and Company E had grays. Futhermore, the trumpeters rode grays; Adjutant William W. Cooke rode an almost white horse; and as a rule, the officers rode horses of the same color as the company to which they were assigned. See General George A. Custer, *My Life on the Plains* (Lincoln, 1966), p. 269; Graham, *The Custer Myth*, p. 346. From the color distribution, we may infer that Eagle Elk had captured a C Company horse which was fastened to one of either I, L or F, all but Company F having been assigned to Captain Myles Keogh. See Hardorff, *Markers, Artifacts and Indian Testimony*, p. 24.

THE MINNECONJOU LAKOTA, WHITE BULL (1850-1947)
This picture was probably taken by F.B. Fiske of Fort Yates,
North Dakota, in 1931 when White Bull was about 81 years old.
Courtesy of National Anthropological Archives, Smithsonian Institution.

The White Bull Interview

Editorial note: This interview was conducted in 1930 by Walter S. Campbell. The interview resulted in nineteen letter-size pages of text, recorded in longhand by Campbell's stenographer, Dallas McCoid, Jr. The interpreter was Sam Eagle Chase, an educated Lakota. The following is a transcript of the original manuscript.

White Bull
Cheyenne River Agency
South Dakota
Summer, 1930[1]

The Sans Arcs was his camp circle. White Bull and his wife lived in this lodge. The wife's name was Holy Lodge.

---

[1] Known among the Lakotas as *Pte San Hunka,* Lazy White Buffalo is perhaps best known to the whites as Joseph White Bull whose life was immortalized by Stanley Vestal in *Warpath, the True Story of the Fighting Sioux, Told in a Biography of Chief White Bull* (Boston, 1934). A Minneconjou Lakota by birth, White Bull was the son of Makes Room and Pretty Feather Woman, and a maternal nephew of the great Hunkpapa, Sitting Bull. The present interview was probably conducted in 1930. It is contained in the Walter S. Campbell Collection, University of Oklahoma, box 105, notebook 23. For additional information on this and the 1932 White Bull interview, see Campbell's biography by Ray Tassin, *Stanley Vestal, Champion of the Old West* (Glendale, 1973), pp. 159-70, 184-85, and also the excellent introduction by Raymond J. DeMallie to the new edition of *Warpath* (Lincoln, 1984), pp. v-xxiii.

She was a Sans Arc. That is the reason for White Bull being there.[2] White Bull's lodge was on the north side of the circle. The one's on each side of White Bull's lodge were relatives. The wife's father was Iron Whiteman.[3]

White Bull got up about daybreak and took his father-in-law's horses up in the breaks. There were forty in all. Eighteen were White Bull's. Five of the eighteen were running horses—four mares and one mule—and the rest were geldings. He took them north of the camp along the river. He took [them] about half a mile from camp. He was watching the horses for a while. About 8 o'clock, White Bull came home for breakfast; then he went back for the horses after breakfast and had his gun and two cartridge belts [with him]. White Bull was trying to head off his horses. They were on the west side. They were about 125 yards from the water.

While he was herding horses, he heard a man yell, and so he went up the river to where the Hunkpapas were, and Sitting Bull was there. They were up to something, and so White Bull started his horses home and got one of his running horses, and he heard guns shooting and saw the women running and yelling, ready to leave.

His father was on the north side of the Hunkpapa camp, and Sitting Bull was on the southside. When the soldiers came to the crossing, they were seen, and by the time they crossed, they had most of the horses caught and White Bull was at the Hunkpapa camp. White Bull was riding a bay horse and [carried] a 17 loading-gun [Winchester]. When

---

[2]Holy Lodge was married to White Bull from 1871 until her death in 1894, the union resulting in the birth of two sons. In 1876, White Bull's lodge consisted of four people: himself, Holy Lodge, their infant son, and a son from a previous marriage with the Sans Arc, Rattle Track Woman. White Bull's matrimonial history included 15 wives, while four times he tried to have two wives at once. See White Bull Interview, (1932), box 105, notebook 24; Tassin, *Stanley Vestal, Champion of the Old West*, p. 167.

[3]White Bull's father-in-law, Iron Whiteman, was a Sans Arc tribal leader and a man held in considerable esteem. See White Bull Interview (1932).

White Bull got to Sitting Bull's place, White Bull's two brothers were there. Sitting Bull said, "Get busy and do something![4]

The first shots of the soldiers went through the teepees, so no one was hurt, but Three Bears was killed down by where White Bull was.[5] When he [White Bull] heard the man across the river, the man had his bay with him and the boy was killed, and this was about three miles from the camp. The boy's name was Deeds. Brown Arse was the boy's father.[6] After Three Bears was shot, Dog with Horns was shot.[7]

---

[4]According to White Bull, "Reno hit camp about 10:30. Horses all out on prairie. Known that soldiers would come that day. Scouts saw them coming at sundance ground. Three scouts, one of which [was] Owns Bobtail Horse. Scouts saw Custer coming three days before [on June 22]." See White Bull Interview, (1932), notebook 24.

Along with the Hunkpapas camped a small number of Blackfoot (Siha Sapas) and Two Kettle (Oohe Nonpas) Lakotas, and although it is generally assumed that Reno attacked the Hunkpapas, he actually hit the Blackfoot whose lodges were pitched on the southern side of the circle. See Interview with Pretty White Buffalo Woman in Graham, *The Custer Myth*, p. 183; Flying By Interview, 1912, Walter Camp Manuscripts, Indiana University Library, p. 348; White Bull Interview, (1932), notebook 24.

This is the first intimation that the Minneconjou chief, Makes Room, may have had three sons. However, the names of only two are known: White Bull and One Bull. The latter, known among the Lakotas as *Tatanka Winjila* (Lone Bull), was born near Bear Butte, South Dakota, in February, 1853, and at the age of four he was adopted by his uncle, Sitting Bull. In 1876, One Bull was married to the Hunkpapa, Red Whirlwind Woman, their assigned lodging place being adjacent to the teepee of Sitting Bull. One Bull passed away on June 23, 1947. He lies buried next to his wife in the mission cemetery on Little Oak Creek, near Little Eagle, South Dakota. For capsule biographies of these two sons of Makes Room, see Stanley Vestal, "White Bull and One Bull—An Appreciation," (Chicago) *Westerners Brand Book* 4 (1947):45, 47-48.

[5]Three Bears was an elderly Minneconjou who died from the effects of a gunshot wound, received at the outset of Reno's attack in the valley. See White Bull Interview, (1932), notebook 24.

[6]Identification of these two tribesmen, and the reconstruction of their activities on June 25, is complicated by a mass of conflicting evidence. A careful screening of the available evidence seems to suggest that they were father and son, and members of the Sans Arc Lakotas. The old man is variously identified by the picturesque English names of Brown Ass, Brown Back, and Pants, while the young boy was called either He is Trouble, Plenty of Trouble, Business, Deed or Deeds. Both of these men were seen near the divide on the morning of June 25 by Lt. Charles A Varnum. Yet, only the father,

A lot of people there together. White Bull does not know [for sure], but he thinks that there were three [Ree] Indian Scouts that took away about ten head of horses.[8] Chased by Owl was killed. White Bull was killed (not this man). When they start fighting, Three Bears [and] Dog with Horns were killed, and after they started for them, White Bull and Swift Bear were shot by a Ree Scout.[9] White Bull does not know the Ree, Bloody Knife.[10]

A Cheyenne was killed after Swift Bear and also by a Ree soldier. White Eagle was killed also.[11] The Ree's name that

Brown Back, would return to the camp sites in the valley—his ten-year-old son was mysteriously slain before reaching the safety of the Indian village. See Hardorff, "Custer's Trail to Wolf Mountains: A Reevaluation of Evidence," *Custer and His Times. Book Two*, pp. 110-11.

[7]Dog with Horns was a young Minneconjou whose reckless conduct resulted in his death from a gunshot in front of Reno's retreating skirmish line. See White Bull Interview, (1932), notebook 24. The death of this Lakota was probably witnessed by the Ree, Young Hawk, who recalled years later that "one Dakota charged the soldiers very closely and was shot about sixteen feet from the line. He rode a sorrel horse with a bald face and his tail was tied [up] with a piece of red cloth." Libby, *The Arikara Narrative*, p. 96.

[8]On the flat on the east side of the river and nearly opposite the present town of Garryowen, six Ree Scouts captured a herd of 27 ponies and 2 mules which they drove onto the bluffs near Reno Hill, hotly pursued by the angry Sioux. See Hammer, *Custer in '76*, pp. 180, 184.

[9]During Reno's retreat from the valley floor, two Hunkpapas, White Bull and Swift Bear, were shot and instantly killed, while the Two Kettle Lakota, Chased by Owl, was fatally wounded. See White Bull Interview (1932), notebook 24. The double slayings of White Bull and Swift Bear may have been accomplished by the Ree, Young Hawk, a very brave, young man only 17 years old in 1876. See Libby, *The Arikara Narrative*, pp. 100-101.

[10]Since White Bull was a Minneconjou, who resided among his Sans Arc in-laws, he would not have been familiar with all the diversified relations of the Hunkpapa kinship units. Bloody Knife was born of a Hunkpapa father and a Ree mother. According to his paternal nephew Has Horns, he was well known among the Standing Rock Hunkpapas. For a biography of this Ree Indian, see Benn Inniss, *Bloody Knife!* (Fort Collins, 1973).

[11]Of the seven Cheyennes killed at the Little Bighorn, only two were slain during Reno's retreat: Roman Nose, killed on the west side of the river near the ford, and Little Whirlwind, killed on the flat on the east side. The Cheyenne slain by the Ree was Little Whirlwind. See Marquis, *Wooden Leg*, p. 268. White Eagle was an Oglala Lakota who was slain near the foot of Reno Hill, presumably by this same Ree.

shot the two Indians was Buffalo Cloud.[12] The Ree was shot down and the Sioux captured the Ree's horse first, and then they went for the Ree and he shot two of them. The Sioux was White Eagle [and] Elk Stands on Hill Top [who] were killed; but they don't know who killed [the] Ree. The Ree that killed Elk Stands on Top was killed right afterwards.[13]

Some of the white soldiers would shoot from the saddle. When the soldiers shot and moved the Sioux back a little, and then they set up a flag, and White Bull said [that] who is a brave man will get that flag. But no one went, and in a few minutes the soldiers came and got it again. The soldiers got as close to the camp as the store from here. These soldiers were not Custer's. When they got off and set their flag and the Indians were about to chase them, and then the soldiers took their run; and there were about three [soldiers] who could not get across [the river] and [who] ran down the west side, and White Bull chased them until the leaders stopped.

White Bull did not kill anything; but he wanted to kill a soldier on a gray horse, but he could not hit him.[14] After they stopped from chasing these three [soldiers], they rest, and Custer was coming but they rest their horses and then started toward Custer, and they shot two of Custer's men before the army stopped.

The women and children were about half a mile [away],

---

[12] Since the name Buffalo Cloud was a Sioux appellation, the identity of this Ree cannot be established. The muster rolls of the Arikara Scouts carry names which are native to the Rees only. Buffalo Cloud is depicted in a pictograph by Amos Bad Heart Bull in Blish, *A Pictographic History of the Oglala Sioux*, p. 212, its text disclosing that the Ree spoke Lakota.

[13] Elk Stands on Top, also identified as Elk Standing High, Alone, Above, or just Standing, was a brave Sans Arc man whose death and the slaying of his killer are depicted in Blish, *Pictographic History*, p. 247. For an eyewitness account of this incident and further details, see the interview with the Oglala, Eagle Elk, in this volume.

[14] This soldier may have been a trumpeter, all of whom were assigned grey horses.

and Custer stopped about straight across from the camp. There were four companies. Custer was in the 2nd from the north.[15] After they were killed, [all] that took a look and (on the map) was where Custer was laying.

The Indians see the women folks, and they stay between the troops and the women. White Bull was on the east end, and White Bull took a center run, but they did not hit him. The second time, he said he was not going to turn back. He charged on the last company. When White Bull start, the rest of the Indians start, and the last bunch run to the 2nd bunch, and the 2nd runs to the 3rd, and all the soldiers get on their horses, and when they [the Indians] were between the two companies, White Bull pulls a white [soldier] off his horse.[16]

---

[15] White Bull's count of only four companies seems to suggest that two of Custer's five troops may have moved together as one unit. White Bull's 1932 interview (notebook 24) reveals: "Where we were standing on side of hill, we saw another [body of] troop[s] moving from east to north where [fleeing] camp was moving, and we charged; it was Custer. We went down east side of the river and we rode straight to Custer. [It] was three miles from where we left Reno to Custer. Chased Custer indefinite distance. Could not see Custer as he was in company. But [it] was about [a] mile from Custer to hill. Still riding in a walking and trotting [pace], still close together. Custer did not stop before they reached [Calhoun Hill?]. They kept shooting as Custer kept moving."

[16] White Bull's 1932 interview (notebook 24) disclosed: "Some Indians went up draw to Custer, White Bull with them—a lot of them. When up in draw, Custer saw them and took shots at them, so they moved back south a ways. Custer at standstill and get off horses to shoot; then get back on [and] made four companies, and one company was shooting at them in the draw. Doesn't know color of horses in [latter] company. On with the battle! After they shoot us back, I left my bunch [and] work around to the east and throw in with another, and now many bunches on south and west took charge at one company and drove them back to where Custer monument [now] is. There was much dust, and we rode among them and pulled them off their horses." The draw mentioned is probably the present Deep Coulee which runs south of Calhoun Hill, and which is not to be confused with Deep *Ravine* which lies to the north of it. Considered a deed of great valor, a "center run" was a mounted display of defiant contempt for adversaries, which solo exhibition served to enhance one's martial reputation. Often possessing powerful medicine bundles, the individuals who undertook such a run had the utmost confidence in their spiritual protectors. For an example of such a Cheyenne individual, see DeMallie, *The Sixth Grandfather,* pp. 190-91. White Bull charged the first company, which was probably L company, deployed on Calhoun Hill, near which White Bull attained his first coup.

When the 1st reached the 2nd [company], they don't run straight. Some run toward the river and they were all killed. White Bull killed a man before he pull the man off his horse. The 4th company went to the 3rd co[mpany] in the draw and they don't go any farther.[17]

Between the 2nd and 3rd [company]—after he pulled the man off his horse—White Bull captured a gun and belt from a dead soldier. White Bull had two 1st [coups]. The 4th co had lost their horses. They had white horses—that was the grey horse troop.[18]

White Bull was chasing horses, and an Indian came in front of White Bull and cut him out. The 3rd company had

[17]The draw which sheltered the third company is undoubtedly the present Deep Ravine which bottom contained the remains of some 28 white men after the battle. Some of the survivors of the fourth company, on the hill, would also in vain try to seek shelter in this same ravine at the end of the battle. Elaborating on the death of his second victim, White Bull recalled in his 1932 interview (notebook 24): "I jerked a soldier off his horse, and after he fell, Crazy Horse counted second coup, and later [he] ran through all [of] them. Crazy Horse [wore] no feather [bonnet]; [he had] loose hair, ordinary hair, face spotted, [and he] carried a gun. Crazy Horse counted coup on White Bull's second [victim]. Crazy Horse ran through infantry [some time] after [having] counted coup and followed by White Bull, from north toward west." The facial painting of Crazy Horse consisted of a red zigzag line and white dots, revered symbols of the hail and lightning powers of the thunder beings. According to his cousin, Eagle Elk, Crazy Horse's hair adornment consisted of a single eagle feather, worn in combat with the tip down, on the back of the head. See Hardorff, *The Oglala Lakota Crazy Horse*, p. 20. White Bull's reference to infantry identifies a company which had lost its horses and which fought on foot.

[18]Company E. was assigned grey horses which are mentioned in nearly every Indian narrative account. For a listing of White Bull's coups, see the editorial addendum at the end of this interview, and also the pictographs in James H. Howard, *The Warrior Who Killed Custer: The Personal Narrative of Chief Joseph White Bull* (Lincoln, 1968), pp. 51-62. Additional pictographs of his exploits may be found in Vestal, *Warpath*, after p. 196, and also in Vestal's article, "The Man Who Killed Custer," *American Heritage* (February, 1957): 4-9, 90-91. Questioned about the spoils of the battle, White Bull disclosed in his 1932 (notebook 24) interview: "(Custer's horses) not fast and did not notice if tired. White Bull got one sorrel, good horse; this was not Custer's; had saddlebags on it, shells and bullets in saddlebags. [He] got good gun. No trouble with cartridges sticking. Had gun been fired when he got it? Yes, empties all. Not many cartridges around soldiers, and [he] got some pistols that had not been used. Many cartridge belts and few used."

bay and white horses at the time, but they soon lost them. Sorrels, bays, and whites were in the 3rd company from the 1st and 2nd.[19]

Before the 3rd company turned their horses loose, they ran south and all except one was killed; but the horse was shot from under him. This might have been the man where the man fought from the hill. Butler must have been from the 2nd or 3rd company, but White Bull did not see him. White Bull did not.[20] Down at Reno there was two soldiers [who] got away, and the Indians killed one and the other killed himself, according to Did Not Go Home, who chased them.[21]

The white men from the 1st and 2nd company were on horseback. They still had their horses when they got to the 4th company, and then they run from the 3rd company and they were all killed down the draw. The last one killed was close to the river.[22] This made White Bull feel good, and he was picking up head feathers right along.

White Bull is going to wear all of his feathers sometime. It is the custom to wear only one or two. Some of the societies, when they would sometime [meet], wear all theirs,

[19]Company C had light sorrels, Company E grays, and Companies F, I and L bays.

[20]Born in Albany, New York, in 1842, James Butler was a first sergeant in company L who had served in the Seventh Cavalry since 1870. Of courageous character, Butler was found on the heights west of Luce Ridge, his mutilated corpse lying amidst numerous cartidge shells. See Hammer, *Men With Custer*, p. 228. Actually, only a few troopers of the third company attempted to escape south. The Oglala, He Dog, told Walter Camp in 1910: "when the [white] men rushed from Custer's last stand toward the river, the dismounted ones took to the gully, and the mounted ones tried to get away to south toward Finley [marker on west end of Calhoun ridge]." See Hammer, *Custer in '76*, p. 207. According to the Lakota, Lone Elk, only nine of these fleeing troopers were mounted, while the Cheyenne, Two Moons, recalled just five. However, only one of these few, Corporal John Foley of C Company, managed to ride as far as Medicine Trail Coulee where luck ran out on him and he allegedly suicided. See Hardorff, *Markers, Artifacts and Indian Testimony*, pp. 29-30, 59.

[21]The individual, Did Not Go Home, has not been identified. Vestal, *Warpath*, pp. 200-201, states that Lt. Henry H. Harrington was this suicide. This is obviously an erroneous conclusion since the incident took place on Reno's battlefield.

and if they shot [an enemy] one, two, or three times they would wear a red feather.

The 1st company was charged by White Bull and his band. The 4th company start to run toward the hill. Most of them don't get to the top, and they lay down and start shooting, and White Bull was on the east side and Crazy Horse wanted to charge. But Crazy Horse backed out, but White Bull went on the run. They were about the nearest horses when Crazy Horse was talking. They were on level ground. He was on the same horse as when Reno came.[23]

When he [White Bull] rode thru, the space was about as close as [a]cross [to] this house. He was leaning on top of the horse, leaning down. When Indians lean on the side of the horse, they would hold both hands on the horse's mane. White Bull has heard that they shot [from] under the horse's neck. He was riding bareback and had a bridle on the horse.

After he [White Bull] goes thru, he joins the group of Indians on the other [west] side, and the 3rd company started running down the hill, and White Bull ran over a

[22]There exists sufficient evidence to conclude that the third company consisted of E troopers and survivors from Companies I, L and C, the latter three originally deployed farther southeast. See for example Grinnell, *The Fighting Cheyennes*, p. 353. White Bull's narrative makes clear that the third company was dismounted, and that it left Custer Ridge well before it was followed by the survivors of the fourth company. The fourth company was probably F Company, of which some 14 troopers had been slain around Custer, a quarter of a mile farther northwest. See Hammer, *Custer in '76*, p.139.

[23]Reference is made to a pictograph drawn by White Bull, but which is not reproduced in this volume. White Bull's statement about Crazy Horse's lack of courage is contradicted by his 1932 interview, in which he stated that Crazy Horse ran through the "infantry" and that he, White Bull, followed him, the movement being across Custer Ridge from north to west. For evidence of Crazy Horse's charge, see the Scott interviews with Red Feather and He Dog, and also the latter's interview with Walter Camp, in Hammer, *Custer in '76*, p. 207, which reveals: "At Keogh [I Company] is where Crazy Horse charged and broke through and split up soldiers into two bunches. Horses stampeded toward river, getting away from soldiers." The charge of these two men may well have been the one referred to by the Cheyennes. See Grinnell, *The Fighting Cheyennes*, p. 351.

soldier on horseback. The Indians got as close as from here to White Bull's house.[24]

The boys keep encouraging each other, saying, "try!" After he ran over the soldier, White Bull's Horse was shot down and White Bull was on foot. Then he saw Bear Lice coming, leading one of the soldiers' horses. It was a bay, and Bear Lice gave White Bull this horse and start again and started for a soldier; but the soldier was shot before White Bull got there, but White Bull struck him.[25]

After he struck the soldier, [White Bull saw] (another) was stand[ing], protecting himself; so he jumped off the borrowed horse and started for him on foot. White Bull was about as far from the soldier as from here to the hall. The soldier was shooting, and White Bull got close and the soldiers threw his gun at him, and White Bull started to fight. White Bull had a gun in his right hand and whip in [his] left hand, and the soldier was trying to knock the gun out of White Bull['s hand]; but White Bull hit him in the neck, and the soldier had on a coat.[26]

White Bull was yelling, so Crow Boy and Bear Lice came over to hit the soldier, and they hit White Bull also [accidentally]. The reason they called Crow Boy: White Bull said, "Hey-Hey, come over and help me!" twice. This was when the man was about to get White Bull's gun. It was the custom to call out when they struck a man. They call, "White Bull to strike the enemy first!" and 2nd, or 3rd. Some [Indians] say to touch this enemy [is] clear enough [indication that the ground rules have been met for earning a coup].[27]

---

[24]The third company retreated to the river sometime after Crazy Horse and White Bull charged across the ridge. This charge may well have stampeded the grey horses. See DeMallie, *The Sixth Grandfather*, pp. 191, 193.

[25]The sequence of the narrative suggests that this action took place in and around Deep Ravine.

After he shot this soldier, White Bull gets his pistol and belt and starts for the enemy, and all that were left were in the draw, and White Bull and his group got in front of the enemy. White Bull saw two soldiers coming, so they [the Indians] got down and waited for them to get closer, and [he] shot one and at the same time a Cheyenne shot the other one. So they both went up and got 1st coup on the one they shot, and 2nd on the other. White Bull got [the] soldier's gun and went up the hill, and when he got up the hill he could not feel his leg; it had been hit, but the flesh was not broken but it was swelling; so he laid in a ditch and laid there until the battle was over and the Indians were going.[28]

---

[26] It was this incident which eventually led to Campbell's conclusion that White Bull had slain General Custer. This belief found expression in the revised edition of *Sitting Bull*, published in February, 1957, and which was followed in the same month by Campbell's article, "The Man Who Killed Custer." This sensational claim did not go unchallenged very long, because the following year Edgar I. Stewart contested its validity in "Which Indian Killed Custer?" *Montana the Magazine of Western History* (Summer, 1958):26-32. The effect of Stewart's provocative article resulted in a response by Reginald Laubin, and a rebuttal by Stewart, the correspondence being published under the editorial caption, "More Rumblings from the Little Big Horn," *Montana* (Winter, 1958):57-61, and which ended with Laubin's rebuttal in *Montana* (Spring, (1959):47-8. However, Campbell was not alone in his belief. In 1968, James H. Howard edited and published *The Warrior who Killed Custer: The Personal Narrative of Chief Joseph White Bull*, which title and contents are indicative of Howard's conviction. Unfortunately, Howard did not examine White Bull's interview notes. Although Custer sported a droopy mustache, White Bull's statement reads that his victim, alleged by Campbell to have been Custer, did not have a mustache! Of Course, this minor detail was omitted from all of Campbell's published works for obvious reasons. However, in view of Campbell's professional reputation, I agree with Raymond J. DeMallie who concluded that Campbell's "motivation was not to deceive, but rather to honor a man [White Bull] whom he had respected in life and whose memory he cherished." See DeMallie's introduction to the new edition of *Warpath*, pp. xxi-xxii.

[27] The individual named Crow Boy has not been identified. He may have been a Crow captive raised among the Sans Arcs.

[28] The draw referred to was probably Deep Ravine. Note that White Bull was going *up* the hill *after* his alleged encounter with General Custer. It seems unlikely, therefore, that White Bull was ever at the monument site where Custer's body was found—during the battle.

With horses brought, White Bull [was placed] on his horse. There were about ten soldiers that chased White Bull up the hill. These were the last ones to live. The fight lasted about an hour, the sun was before noon. There were a few cartridges [left] in the [captured] belts. The soldiers wore caps. They brought White Bull to his father's lodge. Their camp had not been set up. After he got home to his father, Sitting Bull was there and [he] had medicine so he put it on and [took] some buffalo fur and wrapped it up. The announcer said the camp would be there. Some of the women brought their teepees, but some had to go back after them. The medicine was made of root, and it was called "wounded medicine."[29]

White Bull said that [it] was a great battle, and he liked it. During the fight and after the war, the women folks were crying, so White Bull's father announced not to cry but to sing. There is some certain song for the Sioux men that were killed. His father saved a song. The man's name was Elk Stand on Top for whom his father sang. "The people call him Elk Stand, and he was a brave man, but he is all gone now. Sometimes they call him. Elk Stand on Top, they got him for a brave man, but his [spirit] is gone now."[30]

Sitting Bull said to White Bull, "My nephew, you must be careful!—sometime you may be killed." Sitting Bull was

[29]The last survivors seemed to have fled from the fourth company which huddled at the monument site. According to White Bull, ten of these surviving soldiers tried to seek shelter in Deep Ravine.

[30]White Bull's 1932 interview (notebook 24) reveals: "Did not know who white general was. Did not see him. Soldiers not very good fighters, and most were drunk and scared when [they] saw so many Indians. Did not know of whiskey on soldiers, nor smell it afterwards." Asked to comment on the white men's way of fighting, White Bull responded: [They] don't know how to fight. Saw lots of them. Mistakes? [They] should act more lively like Indians; but [they get] too many orders and don't try to save themselves. They stand up straight and run straight—easy to shoot them; half obey orders and half don't (deploying, he means?) Either is just shooting, but in hand-to-hand fighting, Crow [Indians] worse."

across the river fighting, White Bull heard, and [he] did not hear what Sitting Bull did. Indians have an argument: some say Sitting Bull was with Long H[air], and some say he was not there.[31]

White Bull's father was at home watching the women and keeping them together. White Bulls's father was Makes Room [who] was fifty. Then most of the men were young in this battle. Only half of the men went. Makes Room never

---

[31] White Bull's 1932 interview (notebook 24) discloses: "War started about 9 or 10, and lasted till about noon. Never did see Sitting Bull in whole fight. Sitting Bull never told White Bull about his part in fight. When soldiers first came, [did] Sitting Bull take one twin and ride away? Must be so as Sitting Bull and I were there; then I left and did not see Sitting Bull again. Ever know Sitting Bull to be a coward? No. Was Sitting Bull on hill making medicine during battle? No. Just talk. Sitting Bull shot through foot and [it] was not healing right, so Sitting Bull could not run. One reason Sitting Bull not in fight, if not, [was because he] was taking women and children back, then went to fight. One Bull may know." One Bull was White Bull's brother, and he explained (Campbell Collection, box 104, item 11): "Sitting Bull was back on the hill on the edge of the battlefield, sort of directing things tho he himself did not go into the fight at all." During the chaos of Reno's attack, one of Sitting Bull's twins was accidently left behind in the deserted family lodge. This child was later given the name Abandoned One. However, Sitting Bull's biographer, Walter Campbell, took offense at the thought that such an incident could have happened. Seeking to explain the infant's name, Campbell stated that the appellation, One Who Was Left, was given to the child by its paternal granduncle, Four Horns, in commemoration of an incident when he himself was left behind in 1843. See Vestal, *Sitting Bull, Champion of the Sioux*, p. 177.

Convincing as this explanation may be, however, the facts do not support Campbell's conclusion. E. H. Allison, who had married a Hunkpapa woman, had learned the following: "Sitting Bull's own wife had twin babies three weeks old [in June, 1876], both boys. She was so frightened that she forgot she had twins. [She] seized only one and fled with it for the hills, when an acquaintance asked who had the other twin. She then realized what she had done. Passing the child she carried to her neighbor, she ran back to her teepee and brought away the other twin. The one she carried away first was named Yuha Nanpapi. The one left in the lodge was named Ihpeya Nanpapi. The word *Yuha* means to hold, to have, to possess. The word *Ihpeya* means to cast away, to abandon, to lose. *Nanpapi* [means] they fled. So there you have the names of the twins: Fled With and Fled And Abandoned. One [twin], Fled With, is still living and still bears the name given him on account of that event—an unimpeachable witness to the fact that the Indians were taken by surprise and that they fled in fear before the attack of Major Reno's command." Allison to Eli S. Ricker, 3/7/1906, Allison Correspondence, Ricker Collection, Nebraska State Historical Society.

After finding sanctuary in Canada, Abandoned One was named after a tribal chief of

did get in the fight. White Bull never saw Jumping Bull. White Bull never saw [any] chiefs in the fight.[32]

The way White Bull was dressed is [shown] on the picture number 23. [It] is the one where he pulled the soldier off the horse in [the] Custer fight. All he had on was a shirt and medicine [charms]. Number 23 was the first thing he did in the Custer fight. Number 24 is between the 2nd and 3rd company when he got the gun. Number 23 was the one Crazy Horse [counted] 2nd coup. Brave Crow struck on number 25. Number 26 he rode down. Number 27 is the one that got him by the hair. Number 28 is the one the Cheyenne hit 2nd. Number 29 White Bull hit 2nd.[33]

After they bandaged White Bull's leg, noon time came, and after dinner Sitting Bull put medicine on White Bull's wound. White Bull wanted his horse and went back to the battle ground to get his saddle and leggings that he had thrown off; and they went over to where they had been [when] the most close fighting was going on.[34]

Bad Soup pointed at Custer and said that he [Custer] thought he was the greatest man in the world, but there he is. This [Bad Soup] was Sitting Bull's brother-in-law. All of Custer's clothing were taken. This man had no mustache.

---

the northern Black Feet Indians. Known as Crow Foot, this boy was killed by Indian Police in 1890 for provoking hostilities during Sitting Bull's arrest. His twin brother, Fled With, later received the reservation name of William Sitting Bull. He passed away near Pass Creek, Pine Ridge Agency, in February of 1910. See Walter Camp Manuscripts, Indiana University Library, p. 346.

[32]The name Jumping Bull was borne by Sitting Bull's father who was killed by Crow Indians near present Lemmon, South Dakota, in 1859. The individual referred to by White Bull was an Assiniboine captive who was adopted by Sitting Bull as his brother in 1857, and who was later given the honored name of Jumping Bull. Listed on the agency rolls as Little Assiniboine, he and his son, Chase Wounded, were killed by Indian Police in 1890 while resisting the arrest of Sitting Bull. See Vestal, *Sitting Bull, Champion of the Sioux*, pp. 34-38, 301-302.

[33]White Bull's combat pictographs mistakenly show him dressed in leggings. Comparison of the text appended to this interview with the text in Howard, *The Warrior Who Killed Custer*, will disclose variations in the details of White Bull's coups.

[34]Close range combat probably occurred near Keogh's final stand, on Custer Hill proper, and in Deep Ravine.

White Bull got his saddle and leggings and got two pair of [soldiers'] pants. Washed them in the river and brought them home to his father.[35]

White Bull did not see anyone cut up the dead soldiers, but he thinks that maybe some of the parents of dead Indians might have gone up there and did it.

These are the dead [Indians] in [the] Custer fight:

1.	Bear with Horns	Sans Arc
2.	Lone Dog	Sans Arc
3.	Elk Bear	Sans Arc
4.	Cloud Man	Sans Arc
5.	Kill Him	Sans Arc
6.	Rectum	Hunkpapa
7.	Many Lice	Oglala
8.	Red Face	Hunkpapa
9.	Bad Light Hair	Oglala
10.	Hawk Man	Hunkpapa
11.	Young Skunk	Oglala
12.	Left Handed	Cheyenne (Son of Ice)[36]
13.	Owns Red Horse	Cheyenne
14.	Flying By	Cheyenne (Hair People Band)
15.	Bearded Man	Cheyenne. This man made a rush and the soldiers kill him right there. He was killed among the soldiers, and they [the Sioux] thought he was an Indian Scout, so they scalped him and [afterwards] found out they were wrong; and it was Little Crow, brother of Chief Hump who got the scalp.[37]
16.	Black Coyote	Cheyenne
17.	Swift Cloud	Cheyenne

---

[35] White Bull's 1932 interview (notebook 24) reveals: "Where monument [now] stands, another Indian showed White Bull Custer's body; clothing had been taken away and Custer was lying naked. After shown Custer's body to White Bull, this Indian, Bad Juice, [said he] often was with soldiers. Later, White Bull was watering horses and [he noted] one Indian had sorrel horse. White Bull [said]: 'Is that a good horse?' and Indian said, 'I know it is [a] good horse as it was Long Hair's.' Sound the Ground as He Walks [Noisy Walking] had Custer's horse—a Santee, son of Inkpa Luta [Red Top]. White Bull had never seen Custer before; neither other Hunkpapas, nor Sitting Bull, I think." Custer's

These [following] two men were killed by the pack train on the bluffs:

1. Dog Back Bone   Minneconjou. This man was shot about two steps in front of White Bull.

2. Long Road   Sans Arc

These are the ones killed down at Reno in the bottom:

1. Three Bear   Minneconjou
2. Dog with Horn   Minneconjou
3. Chase by Owl   Two Kettle
4. Swift Bear   Hunkpapa
5. White Bull   Hunkpapa
6. White Eagle   Oglala
7. Elk Stand on Top   Sans Arc
8. A Cheyenne was killed, [name] unknown.[38]

They brought all of them to camp and put all the dead in a big teepee. Some were buried other places. They did not

---

body was found void of any clothing, the exception being his white socks and the instep of one of his leather boots. Two gunshot wounds were discovered on the body. One bullet had crushed into the left temple, half way between the ear and the eye, while the second projectile had entered his rib cage, just below the heart. Custer's corpse was subjected to only slight mutilation. In addition to a disfigurement of the genitals, the left thigh had received a knife slash which had exposed the bone. See Hardorff, *The Custer Battle Casualties,* pp. 30-31.

[36] Left Handed was the Lakota name for a young Cheyenne boy known among his own people as Noisy Walking. He died on the evening of June 25 from the effects of a gunshot wound and severe stabbings, the latter inflicted by a Sioux who mistook him for an enemy Indian. He was the son of the respected Cheyenne, White Bull, who was known to the Sioux as Ice. For an account of Noisy Walking's death, see the narrative by his aunt, Kate Big Head, in Marquis, *Custer on the Little Bighorn,* pp. 40-41.

[37] Mustache, or Bearded Man, was the Lakota name for the Cheyenne war chief, Lame White Man, who was killed near the crest on the west slope of Custer Ridge. Hump was a band chief of the Minneconjou Lakotas. The proper translation of his name is High Back Bone (Canky Wakantuya), which means to convey one with a large breast. He probably was the eldest son of Chief High Back Bone, a renowned individual who was slain by the Shoshones in 1870. Of such national tragedy was this incident that it was recorded in nearly every Teton winter count. For Hump's account of the Custer Battle, see Graham, *The Custer Myth,* pp. 78-79.

take their dead with them to White Mountains; but two died on the way and they were buried where they died.[39]

After White Bull came home with his saddle and leggings, then he went [to] one of the bluffs, and staid there all night and came back after dinner and went to sleep; but his father woke him up and told him that something was going to happen. So White Bull went over on the hill where there were some other men, and they told him that a scout told them that some soldiers were coming. So White Bull, Wounded Lice and one other man started out to scout and they saw a soldier and he ran. Then they found some [more] soldiers. They were on the west side of the river, about 9 miles north of the fight. They were horse soldiers and White Bull did not see any more.[40]

They rest a while and watched the soldiers, and he did not scare anyone. Then they saw some horses, and White Bull was leading [in the charge] and they got about thirty head of horses. They went along a short way and then they met a group of Indians, and they were moving because there was soldiers coming, and they were camping at the place where they had the sundance. The Indians asked how

[38]The name of the unidentified Cheyenne is Black Bear. White Bull's list also omits the name of the young Sans Arc, Deeds. A considerable amount of new evidence on the Indian casualties has been compiled by the present author. This information will be published in the near future under the title, *Hokahey! A Good Day to Die! The Indian Casualties of the Custer Fight*, by the Arthur H. Clark Company.

[39]The two Lakotas who succumbed to their wounds are Three Bears, a Minneconjou, and Black White Man, an Oglala. Their remains were sepulchered along Wood Louse Creek near the foot of the Big Horn Mountains. See DeMallie, *The Sixth Grandfather*, pp. 196, 198.

[40]White Bull spent the afternoon and evening of June 25 on the northeast side of Reno Hill where one of the Lakotas, Dog's Back Bone, was killed by Reno's soldiers. On June 26, White Bull encountered the Montana Column near the present Crow Agency. This force of some 450 men was commanded by Colonel John Gibbon who was accompanied by the district commander, General Alfred H. Terry. See the White Bull Interview, (1932), notebook 24. For an excellent review of the march of the Montana Column, see Edgar I. Stewart, *Custer's Luck* (Norman, 1955), pp. 283-307.

many soldiers were there and he said that there was not as many as they had just killed.[41]

So these Indians went on back to camp with these thirty horses. The reason the soldiers did not shoot was that the horses were out of range of camp. After the three got back to camp, they found out that the camp had moved on, so they divided the horses. It was about sundown and White Bull tracked his camp and found some food and ate around a [deserted] tent place, and went on until he found the camp about dark and he heard his father singing: "White Bull, when ever there is a [lot of] people to see you, you do something [brave], and I sure like you." The soldiers were not marching. The horses did not have shoes on. Before they got to home, White Bull met [some] men and they asked him for a horse, but White Bull told him to get some for himself.

White Bull got seven coups. Coup counts if horse hits man. Coups of White Bull:

1. First I saw someone shot one soldier, and as I reached him he fell off [his horse], and I got off [and] counted coup and took his pistol and cartridges, and Indians [were] still charging.
2. One [soldier] had tired horse and was trying to get rifle around to shoot White Bull, but he counted coup and dragged him off his horse.
3. A soldier on foot and pointing gun in all directions. Someone shot him, and I run up and counted coup.
4. Soldier on foot and points gun to Indians; so they could not get him, and [finally] White Bull rides him down and counted coup.

---

[41] Since these horses were unshod, they may have been stray ponies which were caught by the vanguard of the Montana Column, and which were subsequently recaptured by White Bull's party. The Crow Scouts attached to the column do not report the loss of any of their stock on June 26. See the "Journal of James H. Bradley," in *Contributions to the Historical Society of Montana* II (1896), pp. 223-24.

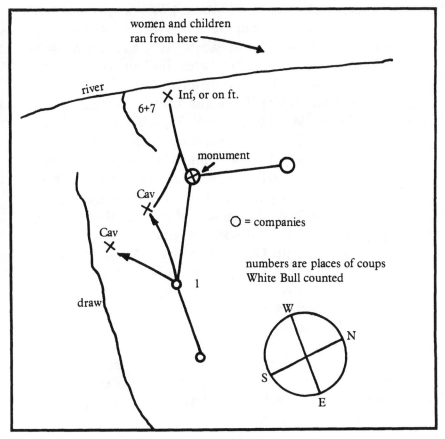

The above annotated map is extracted from a 1932 interview with White Bull, housed in the Walter Campbell Collection (box 105, notebook 24). This map complements the narrative of the present interview, and it is hoped that its inclusion may aid in the better understanding of the combat action on Custer Battlefield. Unfortunately, this map shows only three of White Bull's seven coup locations, and although the circles denote companies, it seems that their final positions have been marked with an "X". Two such positions have been marked with the word "Cav", which, of course, means cavalry, while a third soldier position is indicated by an "X" at the monument. A fourth soldier position is located near the mouth of Deep Ravine, its annotation, "Inf(antry)", indicating the soldiers moved on foot. It is interesting to note that Custer may have advanced some distance past the present monument site, which possible movement receives support from some Cheyenne sources.

5. A soldier afoot, same as [number] "4". Soldier aims [at]
White Bull and does not fire; then, when White Bull gets
close, he throws gun at White Bull, and White Bull
wrestles with him. After [wrestling] so long, [White
Bull] gets on top and hits him on head. Wrestling soldier
tries to take White Bull's gun from White Bull's left
hand, and soldier about gets it. So, White Bull hits him
in face with whip, and soldier lets go. Then, [the soldier]
comes back with fists and hits White Bull on jaw and
shoulder, then grabs his hair and tries to bite White
Bull's nose [who] yelled all the time to scare soldier.
Then White Bull hits him several times on the head and
pushed him over, and takes his gun and cartridge belt
and counted coup. [The] soldier did not make any noise,
and as White Bull was afraid he could not get the best of
the soldier, he yelled all the time to scare the soldier.

6 and 7. Bunch [of] soldiers on foot came in draw, and
White Bull and another [Indian were] ahead and get off
horses, and they fought them and shoot them as they
come. [They] then jump in [draw] and take guns from
them, and more soldiers come; so the two Indians roll
out of [the] stream [bed], or draw, and got away, [having]
counted coup twice.

THE NORTHERN CHEYENNE, TWO MOONS (1842-1917)
This picture was taken by Joseph K. Dixon in 1909
when Two Moons was about 67 years old, and nearly blind.
Courtesy of National Anthropological Archives, Smithsonian Institution.

The Two Moons Interview

Editorial note: This interview was conducted about 1909 by Richard Throssel and was published in 1911 in the columns of the Billings Daily Gazette. *The article contains a short introduction by both the newspaper editor and Throssel, which statements I have omitted from the transcript. It is further known that the translation was provided by Red Water, an educated Cheyenne. The following is a verbatim transcript of the newspaper clipping and includes only the statements attributed to Two Moons.*

Two Moons
Northern Cheyenne Reservation
Lame Deer, Montana
[Summer, 1909][1]

I came to this world in the land of the Shoshone, and on the day I was born a Shoshone chief was killed. At the age of six, a captain came to us and paid us a large annuity on the

---

[1]Born in western Wyoming in 1842, Two Moons was the son of Carries the Otter, an Arikara captive married into the Northern Cheyenne tribe. Although often mistaken to mean the moon itself, the name "Two Moons" merely denoted the Cheyenne way of counting time, meaning two lunar months. This account is contained in the *Billings* (Montana) *Daily Gazette* of July 2, 1911, of which a clipping is filed in the Agnes W. Spring Collection, American Heritage Center, at Laramie, Wyoming. For additional accounts by Two Moons, see Hamlin Garland, "General Custer's Last Fight as Seen by Two Moons," *McClure's* (September, 1898):443-48; Dr. Joseph K. Dixon, *The Vanishing*

Laramie River. Three years later, the Cheyennes started to Horse Creek to get another annuity.[2] From there they started for the Powder River. At that time I was old enough to kill a buffalo calf with my bow and arrow. On their way they encountered a large bunch of Pawnees and there was a big fight, and I remember seeing many of the dead Pawnees as though it was yesterday.[3] Many of these fights made us active on our horses and not afraid. Some two years later we went to the Big Platte River and again received an annuity.

Race, pp. 180-84, which contains Two Moons recollections given in September, 1909. The *Gazette* article was based on an interview conducted by Richard Throssel, an educated Crow Indian living in Billings, Montana. Although its contents suggest the interview took place in the summer of 1909—which is most likely the correct date—a condensed version in the *Billing Gazette* of May 27, 1961, states it was conducted in the fall of 1910. To compound the date problem, the Walter Camp notes at Brigham Young University, at Provo, contain a reworded extract of the Throssel interview which states the date as 1907. In addition to these accounts, the Walter Campbell Collection at the University of Oklahoma Library contains a short, undated interview conducted by Willis Rowland with Two Moons, which probably took place about 1930. The Cheyenne informant, also known as Young Two Moons or John Two Moons, was born in 1855, and passed away in the late 1930s. He was the son of Old Two Moons' half brother, Beaver Claws, who died in 1905, at the age of 87 years. Old Two moons, or Chief Two Moons, passed away in 1917, having been blind nearly the last ten years of his life. See Grinnell, *The Cheyenne Indians,* Vol. I (Lincoln, 1972), p. 104; Campbell Collection, box 105, notebook 15.

[2]Held from September 8 through September 17, 1851, the Fort Laramie Treaty provided for a lasting peace among the signatory tribes and with the whites; recognized the right of the United States to establish roads and military posts in the Indian territory; made depredations by Indians or whites punishable and restitution obligatory; fixed the boundaries of the territory of the respective tribes, but left all the Indian territory open to any tribe for fishing and hunting; provided for the payment by the United States of an annuity of $50,000 in goods for a term of fifty years; declared that violations of the treaty on the part of any tribe would be punishable by withholding a part or all of the annuity from the offender. However, the U.S. Senate reduced the time limit to fifteen years, but increased the annual payments to $70,000. For an excellent review of this council, see LeRoy R. Hafen and Francis Marion Young, *Fort Laramie and the Pageant of the West, 1834-1890* (Lincoln, 1984), pp. 177-96.

[3]After the return of their head chiefs from Washington in 1852, the Cheyennes resumed their wars with their hereditary enemy, the Pawnee Indians of Nebraska. Suffering humiliating defeats in both 1852 and 1853, the Cheyennes and their Kiowa allies gained revenge in 1854 by cutting off and killing 113 Pawnees. See Donald J. Berthrong, *The Southern Cheyennes* (Norman, 1963), pp. 80-81.

At the age of 13, I was a scout for the government, the same as a man, and it was here that I learned much that helped me in after years. We started for Ft. Laramie and while at that place a Pawnee killed my father.[4]

When 16 years of age, we went to war with the Omahas and that made a big fight. The next after that, we came to the head of Pryor Creek and it was here that I won my first coup by killing two Crows that came into the canyon. Three years later I was shot through the leg by a Pawnee while fighting at Cherry Creek, and the next year at the mouth of the Big Horn [I] was shot through the arm by a Crow.

At the age of 23, I was made a chief, and 10 years later I was made the head chief.[5] The next year, or when I was 34, we were out in the western country getting robes and meat. We were not at war with the whites, but were friendly. Word came to us that the pony soldiers were coming after the Sioux. I tried to get my people back to Fort Laramie before the trouble commenced. I wished to miss the soldiers

---

[4]Two Moons' father, Carries the Otter, was slain by forces under Col. Edwin V. Sumner along the Solomon River in Kansas, on June 29, 1857. His remains, along with those of three other Cheyennes, were subjected to extreme mutilation by the Pawnee Indian Scouts attached to Sumner's command. See Grinnell, *The Fighting Cheyennes,* pp. 120, 122; George E. Hyde, *Life of George Bent* (Norman, 1968), p. 104.

[5]There exists some misunderstanding about the political status of Two Moons. It is true that his achieved military rank was merely that of a minor chief of the Kit Fox Society. However, upon the surrender of the Cheyennes in 1877, General Nelson A. Miles took a liking to Two Moons, and on account of the latter's personality and friendliness to the whites, Miles selected him head chief. This selection was approved later by the Cheyenne chief's council, with the expectation that Two Moons would gain favors from the whites for the good of all the Cheyenne people. As expected, the whites spoke highly of Two Moons as a great chief and a renowned warrior. Among his own people, however, he was not considered an outstanding warrior or chief. He took part in the Custer Battle as an ordinary warrior, and he was not mentioned to have merited any battle honors. One contemporary source states that Two Moons chief distinction at the Custer fight was his posession of a Winchester repeating rifle! See Mark H. Brown and W.R. Felton, *The Frontier Years* (New York, 1955), p. 228; Marquis, *Wooden Leg,* pp. 209, 381; Stand in Timber and Liberty, *Cheyenne Memories,* pp. 54, 56.

on the way, for [as] you know, they are never good when they come on marches for that purpose. They do not seem to feel any different towards the different [friendly] tribes like they should. They fight any Indian they run onto.

We were on our way back to the post when one morning the soldiers charged our camp, drove off our horses, and run our women and children into the hills. All the warriors fought back as best as they could with what weapons they caught up in their excitement; but the soldiers burned all our teepees, food, robes, and everything they could find. They fired on all they saw, wounding many and killing some. That broke the friendly feeling we had for them. And our hearts were bad when our babies and children cried from the cold.[6]

A night or two afterwards, my warriors raided the soldiers' horses and got many of the ones they stole.[7] We stayed around them for several days getting as many horses as we could; then we went to where the rest of our people were and all started for the Sioux who camped over on the Platte River. When we reached there we were all nearly starved. Our women and children were almost too weak to travel. It was here, after the Sioux saw what a pitiable condition we were in and had given us food, that we held a big council.[8]

After the pipe [was smoked] I rose and said: "Friends!

---

[6]This was the attack on Two Moons' camp on the Powder River on March 17, 1876, by forces under Col. Joseph J. Reynolds. The dead count amounted to three soldiers and two Indians. For an excellent review of this engagement, see J.W. Vaughn, *The Reynolds Campaign on Powder River* (Norman, 1961).

[7]Of the 700 ponies captured by the troops, the Cheyennes were able to recapture all but some 200 due to the fact that the captured herd was left unguarded. Among other charges, this negligence and the failure to recover the ponies from the Cheyennes led to Reynolds' court-martial and early retirement in 1877. See John G. Bourke, *On the Border with Crook* (New York, 1891), p. 279; J. W. Vaughn, *The Reynolds Campaign on Powder River*, p. 178.

The pony soldiers have fired on my people. They have broken our friendship. They have driven our women and children into the hills to go hungry and cold. They have burned our homes, stole our horses, and now have our hatred. They are coming here to fight you, and we have come to you as friends. Give us arms and horses and we will fight. Give our women robes and food for our children, until we can supply them, and my warriors will fight them to death. Stay with us and we will stay with you. We will fight with you until we are all killed or they are driven back."

Then one after another of my warriors rose and counciled war. It was war, war, war. We wanted our revenge, and it came with Custer. At this great council, such as I have only seen once, all agreed to stay together and fight. We knew we could easily cope with them. The Sioux gave us horses and all the fighting equipment they could spare. We were pretty well provided for and abided our time when we would come in touch with the soldiers on their way again.

We moved our camp and stopped on the lower Rosebud. While here, a messenger came from the south, telling us a bunch of soldiers were coming from that direction (Crook). Another [messenger] came from the east and told us he left the soldiers at Pumpkin Creek. They were under Custer. A council of war was called at once, and we realized that our counsel at the first council was good. All agreed to hang

---

[8]Two Moons was mistaken, because the Sioux were not encamped on the Platte River in 1876. From the Powder River, the Cheyennes traveled northwest down Otter Creek to its junction with the Tongue River; but unable to locate any Sioux camps, they crossed back to the head of Pumpkin Creek. Here, in the breaks, they found a small band of Oglalas who could aid only very little. They then traveled to Blue Mountains (Chalk Buttes), near present Askalaka, Montana, where they found a large village of Hunkpapas who took pity on the Cheyennes. Two Moons Interview, Walter Campbell Collection. See also Marquis, *Wooden Leg*, p. 170, whose account states that the Cheyennes traveled directly northeast without going to Tongue River.

together and fight and not let anyone go away from camp. All had to go in and fight, even if exterminated.

We moved our camp up the Rosebud several days later, after the Sioux had held a sun dance, and went over on the head of what is now known as Reno's Creek. From here all the warriors went back and met the soldiers who came under Crook. We had a big, big fight, and when all was over nearly all the soldiers were hurt. What was not killed went back home. Only three Sioux and one Cheyenne was killed.[9]

We went down to the mouth of the creek and here held another council, and decided not to go back and meet the other soldiers, but to rest and let them come to us. So we moved down under the bluffs where we would have protection from the direction from which the soldiers came. We camped opposite [of] what is now Big Shoulder's allotment. It was here that the other Indians came and told us that Custer was coming and wanted to fight bad. Sitting Bull and his band were camped right at Big Shoulder's place; Crazy Horse and his people were camped just below him, while Elk Head's band were down on the river. The next camp were my people; we were at Medicine Tail's place. These were the leaders and the bands whom Custer fought.[10]

That morning [June 25, 1876] I remember well. We were going to have a dance, but it did not come off. All were

---

[9]This was the battle of the Rosebud, June 17, 1876, during which Two Moons' nephew, Young Two Moons, was saved from certain death by White Shield, a very brave and respected Cheyenne. For Young Two Moons' recollections of this battle, see Grinnell, *The Fighting Cheyennes,* pp. 332-36, and also Stands in Timber and Liberty, *Cheyenne Memories,* pp. 183-90.

[10]Big Shoulder's allotment was near the mouth of present Shoulder Blade Creek, while Medicine Tail's allotment encompassed present Medicine Tail Coulee, across and north from which Two Moons' Cheyennes were camped in June of 1876. Elk Head was the Cheyenne name for a Sioux leader whose Lakota name is unknown.

preparing for all the dancers to gather, when another chief came and told our haranguer to call off the dance. I started to get my horses to drive them to the river for water, and as I went back onto the hills, I looked up the valley and saw a great dust coming. Puzzled over its meaning, I went on and took my horses to the river, then back to the hills from where I saw the fight commence. I realized the soldiers were here, and instead of a dance it was to be a fight.[11]

I rode swiftly to my teepee and told my brother-in-law to go and get the horses quick. Down the valley came the sound of many guns going [off], and the camp begun to show alarm. Old men, women and children were running through the camp. Women [were] leading some of their children and carrying others, while directing the flight of others. The men were hurriedly going to the fight, preparing as they went.[12]

I caught a white horse, and gathering my weapons, [I] started slowly up the valley towards the Sioux camp. I called to the fleeing ones to go slow and take their time, for I would keep the soldiers out of camp. By the time I reached

---

[11] Two Moons' family owned a herd of some forty ponies which was guarded east of the river, north of Two Moon's camp. As early as June 24, the Cheyenne people were warned by Box Elder, also called Dog Stands on Ridge, of the approach of the soldiers. Box Elder, known during his youth as Brave Wolf, was a famous prophet among the Northern Cheyennes who was able to foretell the future. Both he and his father, Horn, gained this knowledge through the wolves, and it was said that both men possessed this power in a high degree. Ironically, in November of 1876, a blind Box Elder predicted the destruction of Dull Knife's village of Cheyennes, but as a result of interference by the Kit Fox Society, the prophecy was ignored with disastrous results. See Two Moons Interview, Campbell Collection; Grinnell, *The Cheyenne Indians*, pp. 112, 223; Stands in Timber and Liberty, *Cheyenne Memories*, p. 215.

[12] According to the 1961 *Gazette*, the name of this brother-in-law was Little Wolf. This individual is not to be confused with the elderly Cheyenne, Chief Little Wolf, who arrived shortly after the Custer battle. Born in 1821, this respected tribal chief was a man of much influence since his early age. He had once been the head soldier of the Elk Society, and as such he had gained a reputation of a dominant war leader who enjoyed the act of killing. Chief Little Wolf died about 1904. See Grinnell, *The Fighting Cheyennes*, p. 49; Two Moons Interview, Campbell Collection.

where they were fighting, quite a number of my warriors were ready and gathering also.

The soldiers [Reno's command] had come to the edge of the Sioux camp, got off their horses and gone into the brush and timber. The Sioux had stopped their charge. I rode in front of my warriors and told them that today we had to win the fight or I would die. Wheeling my horse and calling them to follow, I charged through the soldiers. Then the soldiers went back (retreated) and as they went, one man left the rest and started across the valley in the opposite direction. I followed and knocked him off his horse. The rest crossed the river and started up the bluffs with the warriors all around them. The pack drivers came up at the same time.[13]

I caught a soldier's horse soon after the fight started. It had many cartridges and other things tied to it. There was [a] round can on him, too, and it was half full of whiskey. Soon other warriors began to capture horses, as all was confusion when they ran back to the hills, and all had whiskey cans. But only a few were full, most were nearly empty.[14]

And I went back to quiet the camp, and rode around calling [for] the victory, and telling the warriors to get ready

---

[13]The extracted Throssel interview in the Walter Camp Collection reveals: "As soon as he [Two Moons] took a hand, Reno's men were forced from their position in the timber and soon were retreating. He says that one soldier (Lieut. McIntosh) was having troubles with his horse, which seemed determined to go at a right angle with the direction of the course of the fleeing troops, instead of along with them. In this way, his men easily overtook the soldier and knocked him off his horse with a stone hammer." See also Hammer, *Custer in '76*, pp. 119, 132, which contains additional data on the plight of Lt. Donald McIntosh. The "pack drivers" here referred to were actually the troopers of Captain Benteen's battalion, whose timely appearance on the bluffs may well have averted the complete annihilation of Reno's command.

[14]The reference to alcohol appears only in the accounts recorded in 1909 by Richard Throssel and Dr. Joseph Dixon. However, Two Moons' interviews with Hamlin Garland and Willis Rowland fail to mention this matter.

for the big fight. About the time all were ready and preparing to mount, we saw another bunch of soldiers coming down a draw towards the camp. It was Custer.[15]

Again there was much excitement for we knew we had to fight. We hurriedly crossed the river, and some went up and some down, to get on each side of where the soldiers were intending to come. They came to the edge and stopped; then almost in an instant the guns commenced to go, increasing to a roar like thunder. Custer had started his last fight.[16]

They [Custer's command] dismounted and slowly moved back up the ridge with their horses on the inside and the soldiers around them. We circled around and around. We had them surrounded, and first the Sioux and then the Cheyennes would charge them. In our first big charge, when all swept in together, nearly one whole band was killed. (From the location and the grouping of the markers on the field, it appears [to Throssel] that this was Company I, under Captain Keogh.) I rode back through my men telling them to fight hard and shoot good, and prepare for the next big charge.[17]

---

[15] The "draw towards camp" has probably reference to the soldiers' descent of Medicine Tail Coulee. This revelation is in marked contrast with the interviews given to Dixon and Garland which give the impression that Custer's troops were never near the river.

[16] The extracted Throssel interview in the Camp Collection discloses: "Considerable numbers of Sioux had already gone over the river to the east side at Ford B [Medicine Tail Ford], and as Custer drew near they disappeared into the ravines to the northward. Custer and his men rode up nearly to the river on their horses and were being fired upon by the Sioux posted along the west bank. Here Custer stopped momentarily, and, supposing that they would cross, the Sioux began to appear on his right and rear. He says that some soldiers were killed and were afterwards dragged into the village, dismembered and burned at a big dance that night." This bit of interesting information is not included in the *Gazette* articles, which opens up the possibility that the newspaper account may have been an edited version of an interview possibly conducted in 1907. Walter Camp was a familiar figure at Crow Agency, Montana, where he may have met Richard Throssel (whose Crow name was Esquon Dupahs) and who may have given him a copy of the original interview.

In the next big charge, when we all went in together, they were done fighting in a little bit. The grey bunch were the last killed.[18] Custer was a brave man. I give him credit for attacking a people that vastly outnumbered his—but something was the matter with his men. They did not run nor seek shelter, but stayed right out in the open where it was easy to shoot them down. Any ordinary bunch of men would have dropped into a watercourse, or a draw, where they could have fought for a long time. They acted and shot their guns like something was wrong with them. They surely had too much of that whiskey. That bunch of men should have fought for a long time, but it did not take long to kill them all.[19]

That is all of the Custer fight, and it is just as I have told you; we did not expect to fight that morning. At the age of 36, I came to [Fort] Keogh and took charge of the scouts again. And at 41, with my people, I came to our northern land, and have been here for 26 years. That is all.

---

[17] Walter Camp's copy of the Throssel interview reads: "Custer now turned and charged down the river at Indians who were opposing him, and his (Two Moons') warriors had by this time arrived in large force with their horses. He therefore forded and followed in Custer's rear, the soldiers fighting on foot, in two wings, with the lead horses between them. As Custer passed onto high ground, the Cheyennes split and passed into ravines surrounding the soldiers. Heavy firing was poured into the soldiers from all sides, and as successive charges were made, some part of the troops was wiped out."

[18] The "grey bunch" has reference to Company E which unit had been assigned the regiment's grey horses. See also Two Moons' statement to Dixon, *The Vanishing Race,* pp 181-82, that the grey horses were held on the hill on which the monument now stands, and that successive charges failed to break the soldier line which guarded the grey horses. These statements refute the current theory that E Company was overwhelmend and annihilated *early* in the fight.

[19] In the narrative account to Hamlin Garland, Two Moons vividly described the flight of some 45 troopers from Custer Hill near the end of the fight, which phase he failed to mention in the Throssel interview.

[Editorial addendum: The Two Moons manuscript in the Campbell Collection contains a map of Custer Ridge, which may have been drawn by Two Moons himself. It is appended here because the map and its annotations shed additional light on the movements of the Cheyennes and final stages of the Custer Battle.]

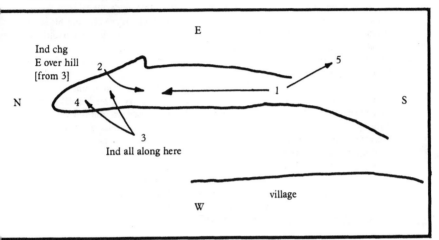

Gray Horse Co. from S on top of ridge

"Walking White" party [made] first charge, side of hill[20]

"Yellow Nose" close by.[21] Both drive soldiers [to] top

Two Moons came [from] NE over hill, yelled, and soldiers ran W down ridge toward river

Cheyennes and Two Moons at "2"

Walking White party and Yellow Nose at "1"

Rest of Indians at "3"

All met at "4" on W side hill. Sixty gravestones here, Custer slightly above. All [stones] in one bunch, covering about one acre; some scattered down valley

Harrington 1 mile toward "5"

Cheyennes from E, and chased SW, then close in on remainder

---

[20] Variously identified as Walking White Man and Crippled White Man, Lame White Man was the head soldier of the Elk Society and a man of much influence among the Northern Cheyennes. At the Little Bighorn, he took a leading part in the assault on Calhoun Hill, driving the surviving troopers in confusion toward Custer Hill. Some

distance southwest of the present monument, he furiously charged amidst the troopers on the ridge and was mortally wounded by a gunshot through the breast. Mistaking the body for that of a Ree Indian, the Hunkpapa Lakota, Little Crow, removed Lame White Man's scalp, while others inflicted numerous stab wounds on the remains. Lame White Man was known among the Oglalas as Bearded Man, or Moustache, which Lakota name hints at the unusual presence of facial hair, which, combined with the meaning of his Cheyenne name, suggests he may have been a captive of white descendants. Although some accounts state that he was an "old man" tribal chief, his age (37) and his active position of war leader would have prevented him from serving in the prestigious office of tribal chief simultaneously. See Marquis, *Wooden Leg,* pp. 211, 242; Walter Camp Manuscripts, Indiana University Library, pp. 366-67, 632-33; *Billings Gazette,* 5/26/1927; Vestal, *Warpath,* p. 199.

[21] Born about 1849, Yellow Nose was a Ute Indian boy who, with his mother, was taken captive near the Rio Grande in 1858 by a Cheyenne war party under Lean Bear. This woman later escaped and returned to her people, but a few years afterwards her daughter, a younger sister of Yellow Nose, was also captured by the Cheyennes. She later became the wife of the Cheyenne chief, Spotted Wolf. Although short of stature, Yellow Nose grew up to become a prominent warrior among the Cheyennes. His battle honors include the act of capturing one of Custer's guidons, which flag he used to count coup on a soldier on Calhoun Hill. After the surrender of the Cheyennes, Yellow Nose settled in Oklahoma where he was still living in 1915, a blind old man with many vivid memories. See Hyde, *Life of George Bent,* p. 297; Grinnell, *The Fighting Cheyennes,* p. 351; Dr. Thomas B. Marquis, *Sioux and Cheyennes* (Stockton, 1973), p. 13.

The Two Eagles Interview

Editorial note: This interview was conducted in 1908 by Sewell B. Weston who based his inquiries on a questionnaire submitted by Walter M. Camp. This interview resulted in three letter-size pages of text, containing 53 typed answers to questions. The manuscript further reveals eight notations in Camp's handwriting, and two notes on separate pages, also by Camp. The following is a verbatim transcript of the original manuscript, to which I have added Camp's questions.

Two Eagles
[Location not given]
December, 1908[1]

Q. Name and age of witness and to what tribe of Sioux did he belong.

A. Two Eagles, 50 years old. Brule.

Q. What chief did he fight under?

A. The band he was with had no head chief; it was

---

[1] Two Eagles was a Brule Lakota who was born in 1858. He was an allottee on the Rosebud Reservation in South Dakota where he was interviewed by Sewell B. Weston in 1908. Weston was a former government employee at the Rosebud Agency who conducted this interview at the request of Walter Mason Camp. The Two Eagles Interview is contained in the Camp Collection, Custer Battlefield National Monument, National Park Service, and it is hereby reproduced with their permission.

everybody for himself. Fought in bands wherever they liked, or mixed in with other tribes where they had relatives or acquaintances.

Q. Were you in the fight against Crook (Lone Star) on the Rosebud a week before the Custer fight?

A. Yes.

Q. How many days were you in the village before the fight with Custer?

A. About 7 days.

Q. How long before the fight was it learned that soldiers were coming?

A. Had just got through with Reno [and] had barely reached camp when Custer arrived.[2]

Q. Did the Indians suppose it was Crook or Custer (Long Yellow Hair)?

A. Thought it was Crook.

Q. Where did the fight with Reno soldiers first begin? At what tepees?

A. Opposite Sans Arc tepees. (He means Custer—WMC.)

Q. What chief or chiefs or what tribes went out to this (Reno) fight?

A. Sitting Bull mounted. Crazy Horse [was] not there when attack was made. (He means Custer—WMC.)

Q. How long did the Reno battle last? Take note of any incidents of this battle.

A. Fight started about 1 P.M. and lasted about 4 hours. Two Eagles states that he was very much excited; that he had just left the women and children who were in tears; that a firm determination came over him. He reasoned that the nation (Sioux) was big and they were going to kill all the soldiers. From this explanation [I infer] it was an intuition.

---

[2]Two Eagles apparently misunderstood the inquiries about Reno because his answers to the next several questions are in reference to *Custer's* attack.

Q. In the Reno fight, did any of the Indians cross the river and try to cut Reno off?

A. Indians were aware that Reno was too well fortified. They had all left him except a few who were watching for soldiers going for water.

Q. After this fight at "R", was there confusion in the village among the squaws and children, and did any of them prepare to leave the village? [See map at page 144.]

A. There was lots of confusion. The women and children started for the hills.

Q. ([Instruction for the interviewer:] In referring to the map, it is presumed that the letters are for the convenience of the questioner, and that to make the Indian understand, it will be necessary to point to the spot on the map.) Where did the soldiers next appear—to the east or the north? (This question is very important. Army officers disagree as to whether Custer came down to the river at Ford "B" and was driven from there to the high ground at "C" [bluff]—or whether he first appeared at "E" [Nye-Cartwright Ridge] and then went from "E" to "D" [Calhoun Hill], and from there to "G" [Custer Hill]. By this [latter] theory he never got to the river at all.) If he was first seen in the east, he must have been at Ford "B". If he was seen approaching from the north, then he probably first was seen at "E" or thereabouts. If there is disagreement about this let me have the exact view of each Indian.

A. Soldiers came down from "E" to a point near "B" and were driven to "C". There were a few [who] went from "E" to "D" [Calhoun Hill]. Those who went from "E" to "D" did so when the main body of the troops went to "B" [ford].

Q. When these soldiers appeared, where there any Indians on that side of the river, and what was their purpose in being there?

A. Two Indians were going up to reconnoiter. [They] were

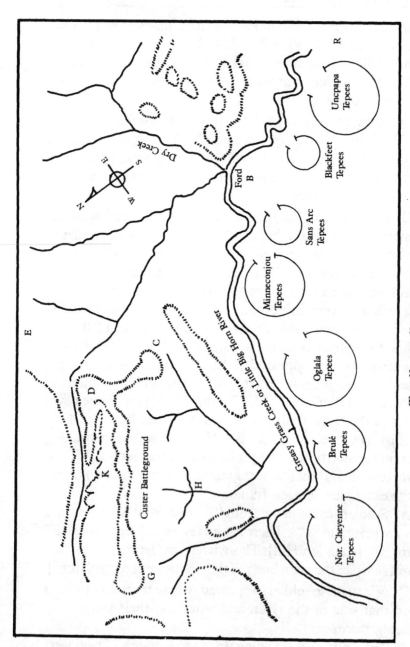

THE CUSTER BATTLEFIELD

Based on a map by Walter Mason Camp. Drawn by the editor of this volume.

going up to see if other than Reno's soldiers were in the neighborhood.[3]

Q. If Custer came to Ford "B", were his men mounted or on foot?

A. All mounted.

Q. Did they get to the river, or across it, or into the village, and was there much fighting there?

A. [Custer] did not get down to the river, [and it was] short fight only.

Q. If Custer came to Ford "B", was he driven off by Indians in great force, or did he appear to be seeking a crossing farther down the stream?

A. At "B", Custer was attacked by a large force, [but I] could not say if he was looking for another ford or not.

Q. If Custer's men went from Ford "B" to "C", did they go in one body or in two divisions?

A. Soldiers were not in a compact body, [and] a few soldiers were killed before "C" was reached.

Q. Was there fighting between "B" and "C"?

A. Yes. (See answers to previous two questions.)

Q. Where did the Indians cross the stream to attack Custer?

A. Indians went anywhere they could find a safe crossing.

Q. Important—When Custer got to "C", did his men all go on to "D" in a body, or did they split and [did] part go to "H" and part go to "D". [Instructions given to interviewer by Walter M. Camp] Try to draw him out definitely on this point.

---

[3]Several men and women observed the approach of Custer's command while on the east side of the river. See, for example, the account of the Minneconjou, Standing Bear, who saw the approach of troops from Black Butte, which was probably the most northern butte of the cluster now known as Weir Point. See DeMallie, *The Sixth Grandfather*, pp. 184-85.

A. Soldiers went from "C" [bluff] to "D" [Calhoun Hill]. Some soldiers on reaching "K" [Keogh's stand] made a dash to the river, [and] went down on a line about half way between "C" and "H" [Deep Ravine]. They scattered some in going down. There were from 10 to 12 in this bunch.[4]

Q. Were there Indians on the long ridge (between "D" and "G") ahead of Custer, or when he got there were all of the Indians behind him?

A. Indians were on long ridge between "D" and "G" before Custer. They came around between "C" and "D" and on the north [side] of ridge and were on top before Custer got there.[5]

Q. Were all of the Indians of the village, that is all of the warriors, were they all [massed] against Custer? Or did some large number of them remain in the river bottom at "R", where the fight first started?

A. There were some at "R". They had neither horses or guns. (These might have been the young men along in front who have given Reno the impression he was surrounded— WMC.)

Q. Did any of the men take a stand and fight hard at "C", or at "D", or at "K", or was there only one firm stand, and that at "G"?

A. "G" [Custer Hill] was the only firm stand made. "C", "D" and "K" was a moving fight.

Q. The men killed between "C" and "D", between "D" and "K", and between "K" and "G", were they mounted

---

[4] A different opinion was expressed by the Oglala, He Dog, who told Walter Camp that "when the men rushed from Custer's last stand toward the river, the dismounted ones took to the gully [Deep Ravine], and the mounted ones tried to get away to south...Line H [Deep Ravine] to C [bluff] mounted soldiers trying to get away when they ran toward the gully." See Hammer, *Custer in '76*, p. 207.

[5] Some of the others interviewed by Weston denied the presence of warriors on Custer Hill ahead of Custer. See the interview with the Minneconjou, Lights given hereafter.

or on foot, and were they making a stand, or killed running?

A. In the fight from "C" [bluff] to "D" [Calhoun Hill] some of the soldiers were mounted and some were dismounted. The most of those dismounted had lost their horses. A slight stand was made at "K". Between "K" and "G" most of the soldiers killed were dismounted and moving.

Q. The men killed between "G" and "H"—were they killed in fighting their way from "H" up, toward "G", at the start of the fight, or in running from "G" toward the river at the last part of the fight?

A. They were killed going from "G" [Custer Hill] to "H" [Deep Ravine].

Q. In the last stand at "G", did the soldiers all fight to the last, or did some try to break away and escape?

A. It was the last of the soldiers (surviving at "G"— WMC.) that run from "G" to "H". They were all dismounted, [and their] horses were either killed or were stampeded.

Q. At what part of the battlefield were you stationed—on the side of the ridge toward the river, or the north side?

A. Part of the time near "D" [Calhoun Hill]. Went around [to] north side of long ridge, and at finish was a little northwest of "G" [Custer Hill].

Q. One company had gray horses. What was seen of them in the fight?

A. The gray horses were not in a body by themselves. They were mixed up with other horses of different color.

Q. Did the soldiers charge on the Indians, and at what points?

A. Soldiers never made a charge.

Q. Did any of the soldiers leave their horses to fight on foot, and where was this done?

A. Soldiers held to horses and stayed mounted until horses were shot and became unmanageable so they were obliged to dismount.

Q. Were many of the horses captured alive, and was there much ammunition found in the saddles?

A. Yes, a great many horses were caught; [however,] more were killed than caught. There was a great amount of ammunition in nearly all the saddlebags.

Q. Were any of the horses taken early in the fight?

A. From the first of the fight horses got loose, [and] some of the Indians would take after [them] and capture them.

Q. Did the Indians hold the top of the long ridge between "D" and "G" during the whole fight?

A. It was a moving fight from "D" to "G". The Indians were in the draws that were just below the crown of the ridge. There were no Indians to the northwest of "G".[6]

Q. At the end of the long ridge, at "G", was the fighting at close quarters?

A. At all times from "D" to "G", soldiers and Indians were quite close to each other.

Q. Custer and 50 men were killed at "G", all on the side of the hill. Why were no soldiers killed on the top of the ridge, where the monument [now] stands?

A. They were killed on top of the ridge. (Two Eagles explains that the top of the ridge was very level, and at the finish, and for some little time before, he was just a trifle north of west from "G".[7]

Q. At what part of the battlefield did any of the soldiers try to get away, and how far did they get?

A. None tried to get away until "K" [Keogh's stand] was

---

[6]This statement is corroborated by the Scott interviews with He Dog and Red Feather given heretofore, which revealed that as little as 40 yeards separated the soldiers on the east side of the long ridge from the Indians on the west side below its crest.

reached. Then, a few started for the river, presumably for water, [and] their manner and progress did not indicate they were trying to run away. It was the 8 soldiers west of "C" [bluff] that came down from "K". (At that time, Two Eagles was on the east side of the ridge at a point between "C" and "D", a little nearer to "D" than halfway between the two points.) (It seems to me that these men might have been sent to see if a way could be opened up for the whole command to escape toward the river, and that they went in skirmish order—WMC.)

Q. Did any of the soldiers escape to the river?

A. None reached the river that he knows of, or that he ever heard of.

Q. How long did the battle last, and where did the soldiers fight the hardest?

A. Battle ended about 5 P.M. The soldiers fought the most stubborn at "G".

Q. Eighteen men could not be found. Could it have been possible that these men got considerable distance from the battlefield before being killed?

A. Could not answer this question.

Q. Were any of the wounded soldiers alive after the battle, and what was done with them? Who killed them—the squaws or the warriors?

A. Almost immediately after the fight, Two Eagles re-

---

[7]The summit of Custer Hill was found to be a nearly level site in 1876, some six feet higher than the adjacent ridge. The laying of the monument's foundation, the digging of burial trenches, and the installation of a fence in the 1880s resulted in the levelling of the elevation, which was measured to be some 30 feet in diameter. The very top contained the bodies of four officers and six enlisted men: General George A. Custer, Capt. Thomas W. Custer, Lt. William W. Cooke, Lt. Algernon A Smith, Chief Trumpeter Henry Voss, Color Bearer John Vickory, Privates John Parker and Edward C. Driscoll, and two unidentified enlistees. Due to the four burial trenches and the placement of the monument, these ten kill sites on top of Custer Hill have not been marked. See Hardorff, *The Custer Battle Casualties,* pp. 33-34.

turned to the village. After he was in the village for a short
period he returned to the scene of the fight. There was one
squaw that he noticed particularly as she had her hair cut
short. (She was mourning for a son killed a few days before
at the fight on [the] Rosebud.) She was carrying an ax,
[and] just before he reached the place where she was, a
soldier got up, but was quickly caught by two warriors who
held him while the squaw killed him with the ax. This was a
private soldier. This squaw was a Cheyenne.[8]

Q. Were any of the soldiers taken to the village alive?
A. No soldiers were taken alive.

Q. Why were none of the soldiers around Custer (at "G")
scalped?
A. It is common among Sioux Indians that when one man
is killed by them it is the practice to scalp him; but when
there are numbers [killed] it is not the practice. This is not a
set rule that is always followed.

Q. Was Custer (Long Hair) recognized during the fight,
or after he was dead?
A. He was not recognized during the fight.

Q. Was Tom Custer (Little Hair) recognized during the
fight or afterward?
A. He was not recognized during the fight.

Q. Was any scout recognized during the fight or after he
was dead?
A. Did not know any of the scouts.

Q. How many Indians were killed or wounded?
A. Can only answer as [to] the number he was acquainted
with, which was placed at 12 killed. The number [of]
wounded was a few more.

[8]There are a number of sources which record mutilations by enraged women. See, for
example, Marquis, *Wooden Leg*, p. 263. See also Hammer, *Custer in '76*, pp. 136-37,
which reports the finding of a bloody ax, "evidently one that had been used by the
Indians to cut up or mutilate the wounded."

Q. How soon after the Custer battle did the Indians leave to attack the soldiers (Reno) on the bluff?

A. The same evening, after the fight with Custer, the Indians made a move on Reno.

Q. Why were the Indians unable to kill Reno and his soldiers like they did Custer's men?

A. From Indian scouts heard that more soldiers were coming; however, they stayed around Reno that night.

Q. Was there any quarreling between Sitting Bull and Gall or any other chiefs during the night after the battle, and what about?

A. Never heard of any quarrel between Sitting Bull and Gall or with any other chiefs.

Q. Why were 30 dead Indians left in the village when the Indians left?

A. Heard that more soldiers were coming, [and] did not think they would have enough time to bury the dead.

Q. Who was the chief of the Blackfeet in the fight? Of the Minneconjou? Who was chief of the Sans Arc (without a bow)? Who was chief of the Brule warriors?

A. Did not know the name of the chief of the Blackfeet. Lame Deer was the chief of the Minneconjous. Yellow Cloud and Spotted Eagle were chiefs of the Sans Arcs. The Brules had no chief. The Brules were mixed in with other bands where they had relatives.[9]

Q. Was American Horse, afterward killed at Slim Buttes, there and with what tribe?

A. American Horse was not there.

---

[9]The Sans Arc named Yellow Cloud has not been identified. White Bull, who camped with his Sans Arc in-laws, recalled the following Sans Arc tribal leaders at the Little Bighorn: High Horse, Black Eagle, Blue Coat, and Two Eagles, the latter probably being Spotted Eagle; see the White Bull Interview, Campbell Collection, box 105, notebook 24, University of Oklahoma Library. The majority of evidence indicates the existence of a Brule camp whose lodges were erected adjacent to the Oglala circle. See the Hollow Horn Bear interview given hereafter.

THE OGLALA LAKOTA, LONE BEAR
This picture was taken by Heyn and Matzen of Omaha, Nebraska,
ca. 1900, when Lone Bear was about 53 years old.
Courtesy of National Anthropological Archives, Smithsonian Institution.

The Lone Bear Interview

Editorial note: This interview was conducted in 1909 by Sewell B. Weston who based his inquiries on a revised questionnaire submitted by Walter M. Camp. The interview resulted in three letter-size pages of text, containing 61 typed answers to questions. The manuscript further reveals one notation in Camp's handwriting. Appended to this manuscript is a short note by Weston to Camp in reference to the informant. The following is a verbatim transcript of the original manuscript, to which I have added Camp's questions.

Lone Bear
Cody, Wyoming
January 5, 1909[1]

Q. Name and age and to what tribe of Sioux did you belong?
A. Lone Bear (Mato Wajila). 61 years old. Oglala.

---

[1] Lone Bear was an Oglala Lakota who was born about 1847. It was said of him that he had cut off the tongue of one of Reno's wounded troopers, and that he kept this grizzly momento the remainder of his life. After the surrender of the hostiles in 1877, he enlisted in the U.S. Indian Scouts and was transferred later to the Pine Ridge Indian Police. In this capacity he faithfully served the white authorities for more than twenty years. The Lone Bear interview was conducted by Sewell B. Weston in 1909 at the request of Walter M. Camp. It is presently contained in the Camp Collection, Custer Battlefield National Monument, National Park Service, and it is hereby reproduced with their permission.

Q. What chief did he fight under?

A. Crazy Horse (Tasunka Witko).

Q. Were you in the fight against Crook?

A. Yes.

Q. When the Sioux fought Crook, where was the village? How far from the battle with Crook?

A. The Indian village was a long way from the place of the battle. The battle was near the mouth of [the] Rosebud, in a shallow canyon in which the fallen timber was thick.

Q. How many days were you in the village before the fight with Custer?

A. Four or five days.

Q. On the map, [do] I have the tribes in the village in the proper order? Beginning at the south end: Uncpapa, Blackfeet, Sans Arc, etc.? How many tepees, warriors and people in village of your tribe?

A. Yes, [order is correct]. Except there were a few tepees occupied by some Arapahoes, situated between the Oglalas and Brules.[2] It was impossible for him to estimate the number of warriors or tepees—just "lela ota" (a great many).

Q. How long before the fight was it learned that soldiers were coming?

A. The warriors were taken by surprise.

Q. Did the Indians suppose it was Crook or Custer that was coming?

---

[2]The number of Arapahoes present at the Little Bighorn amounted to a war party of only six young men who had left Fort Robinson in Nebraska on a foray against the Shoshones. While enroute, they were discovered and detained by the Sioux who suspected them to be scouts for the U.S. Army. However, through the intervention of the Cheyennes—particularly Two Moons who had Arapahoe relatives—these six captives were released and they subsequently took part in the Custer Battle. The accounts of two of these men may be found in Graham, *The Custer Myth*, pp. 109-112. See also Marquis, *Wooden Leg*, p. 204, which states that the Arapahoes alleged to have killed a white man on Powder River—which may have been a ploy to convince the Sioux of their loyalty.

A. None of the warriors knew it was Custer.

Q. Where did the fight with Reno's soldiers first begin? At what tepees?

A. At the Uncpapa tepees. Reno was under the impression there were only a few tepees, just what could be seen [from] on top of the knoll.

Q. How long did Reno's battle last? Take note of any incidents of this battle.

A. From 9 to 11 A.M. There was nothing of note to be gained from the witness as he never got very near to the front in this fight.

Q. In this fight did any of the Indians cross the river and try to cut Reno off?

A. There was no attempt made to cut Reno off that he saw.

Q. Where did the soldiers next appear—to the east or the north?

A. They came from the northeast and were first seen coming down from "E" [Nye-Cartwright Ridge].

Q. When these soldiers appeared, were there any Indians on that side of the river, and what was their purpose in being there?

A. Did not see any Indians on north side of river.

Q. If Custer came to Ford "B", were his men mounted or on foot?

A. Soldiers were dismounted and were leading their horses.

Q. Did they [Custer] get to the river, or across it, or into the village, and was there much fighting there?

A. The soldiers never got to the river.

Q. If Custer came to Ford "B", was he driven off by Indians in great force, or did he appear to be seeking a crossing farther down the stream?

A. The warriors started after Custer before he reached the

river. Some of the Indians were mounted and some on foot. They crossed the river in bunches, large numbers crossing at "B". Others crossed where a safe crossing could be made.

Q. If Custer's men went from Ford "B" to "C" [bluff], did they go in one body or in two divisions?

A. About this time, witness returned [to his lodge] for his horse. On his return the soldiers were all at a point near "C" and in a body.

Q. Was there fighting between "B" and "C"?

A. Witness heard considerable shooting while he was after his horse.

Q. Where did the Indians cross the stream to attack Custer?

A. Most of the Indians crossed at "B"; some crossed down the stream.

Q. (Important—WMC.) When Custer got to "C", did his men all go on to "D" [Calhoun Hill] in a body, or did they split up, and part go to "H" [Deep Ravine] and part to "D"?

A. The soldiers all went to "D". On this point the witness was very emphatic.

Q. Were there Indians on the long ridge (between "D" and "G" [Custer Hill]) ahead of Custer, or, when he got there, were all of the Indians behind him?

A. Witness [is] not clear as to Indians being on long ridge before Custer or not. There were many Indians behind him.

Q. Were all the Indians of the village, that is, all of the warriors, were they all against Custer? Or did some large number of them remain in the river bottom at "R", where the fight first started?

A. All of the warriors were against Custer. There could have been some at "R", but he did not know of any. Many squaws were back of the Indians.

Q. Did any of the men make a stand and fight hard at "C" or at "D", or at "K", or was there only one firm stand, and that at "G"?

A. There was a short stand made at "C" [bluff] and "D" [Calhoun Hill]. Witness thinks the longest stand and the hardest fighting was done at "K" [Keogh's stand]. At this point many of the horses were killed. He seems to think a longer stand was made at "K" than at "G" [Custer Hill].

Q. The men killed between "C" and "D", between "D" and "K", and between "K" and "G", were they mounted or on foot, or were they making a stand or killed running?

A. From "C" [bluff] to "G" [Custer Hill] most of the men were dismounted and using their horses as shields. The soldiers were moving most of the time. Once in a while they would make a short stand.

Q. The men killed between "G" and "H"—were they killed in fighting their way from "H" up toward "G", at the start of the fight, or in running from "G" toward the river at the last part of the fight.

A. These men were killed going from "G" [Custer Hill] to "H" [Deep Ravine] at the last stages of the fight.

Q. Were any men killed in the deep gully at "H"? How many? Just a few, or a good many?

A. Witness did not get down that far. He stopped near where Dr. Lord is shown on the map.[3]

Q. In the last stand at "G", did the soldiers all fight to the last or did some try to break away and escape?

A. Soldiers were fighting hard at "G" [Custer Hill]. There were a few who tried to get away.[4]

Q. One company had gray horses. What was seen of them in the fight?

A. At "C" all horses were mixed up.

Q. At what part of the battlefield were you stationed—on the side of the ridge toward the river, or on the north side?

A. At first he was on the north side of [the] long ridge, [and] later crossed to the south side at a point about half way between "K" [Keogh's stand] and "G" [Custer Hill].

Q. Did the soldiers charge on the Indians, and at what points?

A. Soldiers never made a charge during the entire fight.[5]

Q. Did any of the soldiers leave their horses to fight on foot, and where was this done?

A. A great many of the soldiers were dismounted all along during the fight.

Q. Were many of the horse captured alive, and was there much ammunition in the saddles?

A. A great many of the horses were captured. Considerable ammunition was found in the saddlebags.

Q. Were any of the horses taken early in the fight?

---

[3]Born in Boston, Massachusetts in 1846, First Lieutenant George E. Lord was an assistant surgeon who accompanied the Seventh Cavalry on the ill-fated campaign in 1876. He was last seen alive with Custer's battalion at noon, June 25, and although rumors suggest that his remains were identified on June 27, the official reports list him as missing in action and presumed killed. See Hammer, *Men with Custer*, p. 9, and also the report of Captain Michael V. Sheridan, dated 7/20/1877, in Graham, *The Custer Myth*, p. 374. Years later some distinctive buttons worn only by medical personnel were discovered near Deep Ravine and accordingly Dr. Lord's marker was placed at this location in 1890. See Hammer, *Custer in '76*, p. 252.

[4]The troopers who attempted to escape from Custer Hill at the very end of the fight have been estimated by various witnesses at less than ten. See Marquis, *Wooden Leg*, p. 237, and also Vestal, *Sitting Bull, Champion of the Sioux*, p. 171.

[5]For a different opinion, see the account of the Lakota, Red Horse, who stated that Custer's soldiers made five brave stands; that the rear guard charged the Indians who then scattered; but that many of the white men became foolish and threw down their weapons, asking for pity. See Graham, *The Custer Myth*, pp. 60, 62.

A. No horses were taken until after the soldiers reached "C".

Q. Did the Indians hold the top of the long ridge between "D" and "G" during the whole fight?

A. Yes, during the entire fight.

Q. How long did the battle last, and where did the soldiers fight hardest?

A. The battle lasted from about noon until 4 o'clock. The fighting was the hardest at "K".

Q. At the end of the long ridge, at "G", was the fighting at close quarters?

A. Yes, at close quarters. Indians pulled some of the soldiers who were mounted off their horses.

Q. Custer and 50 men were killed at "G", all on the side of the hill. Why were no soldiers killed on the top of the ridge, where the monument [now] stands?

A. Soldiers were killed on the side of the hill at "G". Witness states that soldiers made a stand there (on the top) for just a short time and were [then] forced over the hill.

Q. At what part of the battlefield did any soldiers try to get away, and how far did they get?

A. At "G" [Custer Hill]. That point was the first and only place where the soldiers tried to get away, and only a few [from] there.

Q. Did any soldiers escape to the river?

A. No soldier got as far as the river so far as witness knows or ever heard.[6]

Q. Eighteen men could not be found. Could it have been

---

[6] Survivors of the Reno-Benteen force claim to have seen the remains of troopers on the west bank of the river, across from Deep Ravine. The validity of these statements is supported by the Hunkpapa, Gall, who asserted in 1886 that several soldiers had crossed the river to the west bank but were killed during the attempted escape. *St. Paul Pioneer Press,* 7/16/86.

possible that these men got considerable distance from the battlefield before being killed?

A. Do not know what became of the 18 men. Never heard of any getting away.[7]

Q. Were any of the wounded soldiers alive after the battle, and what was done with them? Who killed them—the squaws or the warriors?

A. Yes, there were numbers of soldiers wounded and alive after the fight. They were mostly killed by the squaws who followed the warriors in the fight.

Q. Were any soldiers taken to the village alive?

A. No soldiers were taken alive.

Q. Why were none of the soldiers around Custer (at "G") scalped?

A. Does not know why they were not scalped. They stripped them of their clothing instead.

Q. Was Custer (Long Hair) recognized during the fight or afterward?

A. No, Custer was not recognized during the fight.

Q. Was Tom Custer (Little Hair) recognized?

A. No.

Q. Was any scout recognized?

A. No.

---

[7] Since the muster rolls of the five companies slain with Custer were not recovered, it was not found out until the regiment's return to Fort Lincoln how many of these men were actually alive due to sickness and detached service at the outset of the campaign. This problem was further compounded by the fact that the dead count obtained on June 28 did not include the bodies found years later near Medicine Tail Coulee and Deep Coulee. It comes as no surprise, therefore, that the Army was faced with the problem of unaccounted personnel, which probably gave rise to the rumor that these "missing" soldiers had fled the battlefield, to be trapped some distance east near the foot of the Wolf Mountains. Although this rumor was eventually discounted, it was still evident a year later when it found expression in Sheridan's Official Report. See Hardorff, *Markers, Artifacts and Indian Testimony,* pp. 29-30, 37-38; Graham, *The Custer Myth,* p. 374. For an excellent analysis of the combat strength and fatalities of Custer's regiment, see Gray, *Centennial Campaign,* pp. 284-97.

Q. How many Indians were killed or wounded.

A. 30 killed and 5 more died of their wounds sometime after.

Q. How soon after the Custer battle did the Indians leave to attack the soldiers (Reno) on the bluff?

A. The same night.

Q. Why were the Indians unable to kill Reno and his soldiers?

A. Reno had thrown up breastworks. He was too firmly entrenched.

Q. Was there any quarreling between Sitting Bull and Gall?[8]

A. None that he heard of.

Q. Why were 30 dead Indians left in the village when the Indians left?

A. Thought more soldiers were coming.

Q. Who were the chiefs?

A. The only chief he knew in the entire outfit was Sitting Bull (and Crazy Horse).

Q. Was American Horse, afterward killed at Slim Buttes, there?

A. American Horse was not there.[9]

Q. When the soldiers arrived at "G", did many of them have their horses?

A. Some of them had horses at "G", [but] about half that had horses had turned them loose at this point. He does not know why this was done.

Q. How long did the battle at "G" last? If a long time, why so long? Did the soldiers there run out of ammunition before the Indians closed in on them?

----

[8] Some scholars contend that the relationship between these two Hunkpapas was strained due to political aspirations. Although this may have been the case during the reservation years, apparently no such friction existed, if ever, prior to this time.

A. There was a good stand made at "G" [Custer Hill], [but] not so long or as firm as the one made at "K" [Keogh's stand]. The ammunition found on the men at "G" was not plenty.

Q. Did the soldiers who ran from "G" toward "H" have their guns and ammunition?

A. Yes they had their guns.

Q. Were any of the soldiers seen to commit suicide or to shoot each other when finally surrounded?

A. One man committed suicide. Did not see any soldiers shoot each other.

---

[9]According to the Hunkpapa, Has Horns, and others, the Lakota shot through the bowels at Slim Buttes was a Sans Arc who was known among his own people by the name of Iron Shield. He was a respected individual, but not a tribal leader. There were, however, two Oglalas named American Horse. One was the tribal leader of the True Oglala Band of the Southern Oglalas. His father was Sitting Bear, known also in his younger days as American Horse, who was the keeper of the tribal winter count. The second American Horse was the son of Old Smoke and the leader of a wild band of Northern Oglalas. Neither one of these two Oglala leaders was slain at Slim Buttes and apparently were not even present when this engagement took place. Thus, the question asked about the death of American Horse must have puzzled Weston's informants. See the Has Horns Interview, Camp Manuscripts, p. 357, Indiana University Library; Hammer, *Custer in '76.* p. 208; Hyde, *Red Cloud's Folk,* p. 318.

The Lights Interview

Editorial note: This interview was conducted in 1909 by Sewell B. Weston who based his inquiries on a questionnaire submitted by Walter M. Camp. This interview resulted in four letter-size pages of text, containing 63 typed answers to questions. The following is a verbatim transcript of the original manuscript, to which I have added Camp's questions.

Lights
[Location not given]
Spring 1909[1]

Q. Name and age and to what tribe of Sioux did you belong?
A. Light (Cragre), or Runs after the Clouds (Mahpiyah Luwa Isaye [Chases Red Clouds]), 56 years. Minneconjou.
Q. What chief did he fight under?

---

[1] Lights was a Minneconjou Lakota who was born about 1853. His nickname may have been derived from his formal name which actually translates into Chases Red Clouds, meaning the arrival of daylight. This interview was arranged by Sewell B. Weston at the request of Walter M. Camp, and like the other Weston interviews it was probably conducted through the services of A. G. Shaw of Valentine, Nebraska, who interpreted for a number of pioneer field researchers. The Lights Interview is contained in the Camp Collection, Custer Battlefield National Monument, National Park Service, and it is hereby reproduced with their permission.

A. Spotted Elk. (He was under several. Spotted Elk was his main chief.)[2]

Q. Were you in the fight against Crook on the Rosebud a week before the Custer fight?

A. Was in the fight with Crook on the Rosebud.

Q. How many days were you in the village before the fight with Custer?

A. Four or Five days.

Q. How long before the fight was it learned that soldiers were coming?

A. Short time before the arrival of soldiers, some Indians that were out returned and reported seeing clouds of dust northeast and east. They were not in camp long before Custer and his men appeared.

Q. Did the Indians suppose that it was Crook or Custer that was coming?

A. Did not know who it was.

Q. Where did the fight with Reno first begin? At what tepees?

A. With the Uncpapas. (Sitting Bull tepees.)

Q. What chief or chiefs or what tribes went out to Reno's fight?

A. Sitting Bull's outfit and some stragglers from other tepees. Could not state who led the Indians.

Q. How long did Reno's battle last? Take note of any incidents of this battle.

A. Fight started about 9:30 A.M. [and] lasted nearly until noon. This witness had a comrade who was shot in the head south of the high ridge. He stopped there to look after his

---

[2] Spotted Elk was one of four sons born to the Minneconjou leader Lone Horn. Better known as Big Foot, he was slain with some 150 of his followers at Wounded Knee, South Dakota, on December 29, 1890. For a classic study of this regrettable affair, see Robert M. Utley, *The Last Days of the Sioux Nation*, (New Haven, 1963).

friend. (This must have happened in front of Reno's skirmish line—WMC.)

Q. In Reno's fight did any of the Indians cross the river to try to cut him off?

A. No one got ahead of Reno in his retreat. Lights was well in front when his comrade was shot. He did not proceed any farther than stated in the previous question.

Q. After the fight at "R", was there confusion in the village among the squaws and children, and did any of them prepare to leave the village?

A. Yes, considerable confusion. Excitement was intense. Women and children scattered down the stream and up in the hills.

Q. Where did the soldiers next appear—to the east or to the north?

A. They were first seen at a point near "E" [Nye-Cartwright Ridge].

Q. When these soldiers appeared were there any Indians on that side of the river, and what was their purpose in being there?

A. None that he knows of.[3]

Q. If Custer came to Ford "B", were his men mounted or on foot?

A. They all appeared to be dismounted. They got to within a quarter of a mile of "B" [river]. That was as near as they ever got to the river.[4]

---

[3] A small party of Cheyennes had left the encampment on a foray against tribal enemies, and on reaching a location east of Custer Hill, near present U.S. Highway 212, their attention was attracted by troops near Medicine Tail Coulee. One of these Cheyennes was Wolf Tooth whose experiences are related by his step-grandson, Stands in Timber, in *Cheyenne Memories*, pp. 197-98.

[4] According to Sioux and Cheyenne sources, the initial opposition confronting Custer on the east bank near the ford may have been less than twenty warriors. See Grinnell, *The Fighting Cheyennes*, p. 350; Hammer, *Custer in '76*, p. 207.

Q. Did they get to the river?

A. See previous question.

Q. If Custer came to the ford, was he driven off by the Indians in great force?

A. See previous answer. The Indians were swarming out of their tepees in such great numbers that he [Custer] appeared to be looking out for the safety of his men more than he did for a chance to cross the river at some other point than at "B". (That is to say, Custer hesitated when he saw the odds against him—WMC.)

Q. If Custer's men went from Ford "B" to "C" [bluff], did they go in one body or in two divisions?

A. They were in company formation and apparently in good order.

Q. Was there fighting between "B" and "C"?

A. Yes, there was a continual fight from where Custer first stopped back to "C"—not very vigorous, but shooting was indulged in by both soldiers and warriors.

Q. Where did the Indians cross the stream to attack Custer?

A. At any place where they could find a convenient and safe crossing.

Q. (Important!) When Custer got to "C" did his men all go on to "D" in a body, or did they split up and part go to "H" and part to "D" [Instructions given to interviewer by Walter M. Camp] Try to draw him out definitely on this point.

A. All went from "C" [bluff] to "D" [Calhoun Hill]. (The witness was very positive on this point as he was just to the northeast of "C" and had a good command of the entire ridge between the two points mentioned.)

Q. Were there Indians on the long ridge (between "D"

and "G") ahead of Custer, or when he got there, were all of the Indians behind him?

A. There were none in front. At "C" [bluff] they were on both sides of him.

Q. Were all of the Indians of the village, that is, all of the warriors, were they all against Custer? Or did some large number remain in the river bottom at "R", where the fight first started?

A. He does not know of any warrors being at "R". Thinks they were all out against Custer.

Q. Did any of the men make a stand and fight hard at "C" or at "D" or at "K", or was there only one firm stand, and that at "G"?

A. He is not very positive about any stand being made at "K" [Keogh's stand]. If there was a stand made it was short. The only stand of any great length was at "G" [Custer Hill]. At "C" [bluff] and "D" [Calhoun Hill] the soldiers were moving

Q. The men killed between "C" and "D", between "D" and "K", and between "K" and "G", were they mounted or on foot, and were they making a stand or killed running?

A. They were most[ly] all mounted. The soldiers who were afoot either had their horses shot or were stampeded. [The soldiers were] killed fighting [and] did not seem to be running away, only giving ground by reason of superior numbers.

Q. The men killed between "G" and "H"—were they killed in fighting their way from "H" up toward "G", at the start of the fight, or in running from "G" toward the river at the last part of the fight?

A. [They] were fighting from "G" [Custer Hill] to "H" [Deep Ravine] at last of fight.

Q. In the last stand at "G" did the soldiers all fight to the last, or did some try to break away and escape?

A. Some of them tried to get away by jumping over the high banks at places between "G" and "H".

Q. At what part of the battlefield were you stationed?

A. This witness went around the north and west side of the long ridge, to a point west of "G", being nearer to "G" than to "H". The fighting was a little too warm for him there, and he moved down nearer to "H" and was there at the finish. It was at this latter place that he saw a few of the soldiers jump over the banks.[5]

Q. One company had gray horses. What was seen of them in the fight?

A. One company had gray horses. In the retreat around to about "K" they were in the fighting front. At that point they were mixed up with the other horses. At this point the companies would alternate in covering the retreat of the others. (First one squad and then another would try to cover the retreat—WMC.)

Q. Did the soldiers charge at the Indians, and at what points?

A. The soldiers never made a charge.

Q. Did any of the soldiers leave their horses to fight on foot, and where was this done?

A. No, the soldiers who were mounted kept their horses until it was shot from under him, stampeded or taken away by the warriors.

---

[5] The Hunkpapa, Good Voiced Elk, was also near the head of Deep Ravine, and he recalled that "those who broke from [the] end of ridge and tried to get away by running toward the river were dismounted. There was a deep gully without any water in it. I saw many jump over the steep bank into this gully in their effort to escape, but these were all killed. There were probably 25 or 30 of them." See Walter M. Camp Papers, Robert S. Ellison Collection, item 6, Denver Public Library.

Q. Were many of the horses captured alive, and was there much ammunition found in the saddles?

A. Yes, many were caught, [and] all had plenty of ammunition in the saddles.

Q. Were any of the horses taken early in the fight?

A. Yes, some were caught early in the fight, [but] many were wounded however.

Q. Did the Indians hold the top of the long ridge between "D" and "G" during the whole fight?

A. Yes, the warriors kept the long ridge all through the fight, i.e., they kept the soldiers on the top of the ridge.[6]

Q. How long did the fight last, and where did the soldiers fight the hardest?

A. Witness states that after the fight with Custer he went back to camp and caught another horse and went after Reno. The sun was still up. Witness had no idea as to time measured by minutes and hours.

Q. At the end of the long ridge, at "G", was the fighting at close quarters?

A. Yes, near enough to look each other in the eyes. Between "G" [Custer Hill] and "H" [Deep Ravine] the warriors were taking the guns away from the soldiers. Also, the soldiers, in running away, became so demoralized that they would fire in the air, making them easy victims when they were caught. (Presumably they had fired and [had] not stopped to load—WMC.)[7]

---

[6]The geographical limitations of Custer Ridge in 1876 would have prohibited its occupation by troops. Present-day visitors who travel over Custer Ridge do so by means of a blacktop which surface amply facilitates its motorized traffic. Yet, in 1876, this very ridge was a hogback, its top less than three feet wide, which narrow surface did not allow combat deployment and, therefore, it could not have contained firing refuse. It was not until 1934 that a road was laid out. This work required the razing of several hillocks, while at the same time the crest of the ridge was lowered several feet to widen its top. Thus, the fact that the ridge had been a hogback, combined with the disturbance of its top, may explain the lack of any situs artifacts.

Q. Custer and 50 men were killed at "G", all on the side of the hill. Why were no soldiers killed on top of the ridge, where the monument [now] stands?

A. Witness states that many of the soldiers were killed on the top of the ridge where the monument stands. Those killed on the side of the ridge were trying to make their escape.

Q. At what part of the field did any soldiers try to get away, and how far did they get?

A. Soldiers tried to get away when they reached "G" [Custer Hill]. There was one who tried to get away by going north at "K" [Keogh's stand], [but] he did not get very far.[8]

Q. Did any of the soldiers escape to the river?

A. None that the witness personally knows of. Hearsay: one soldier was found some days after[wards] and many miles away. Wounded, he had been subsisting on raw frogs and some were found in his pockets after he was killed. Hearsay: the body of man wearing a buckskin suit and who resembled Tom Custer was first found about a quarter of a mile west of the ridge marked "C" [bluff] and who was afterward carried up and placed at "G" [Custer Hill].[9]

Q. Eighteen men could not be found. Could it have been

[7]This erratic behavior by the troops during the final phase of the battle was commented on by a number of informants. Two Minneconjous, One Bull and White Bull, told Walter Camp that those who ran down the ridge had discarded their carbines and used revolvers instead. This statement is corroborated by the Oglala, Bear Lying Down, who asserted further that some of these soldiers were firing in the air, firing wildly without taking aim, acting as if they were intoxicated. However, the Oglala, He Dog, made clear that none of these soldiers were drunk, but he added that some of them had played possum, which was considered a rather foolish thing to do when fighting Indians. See Camp Manuscripts, pp. 126-27, 269, 350, Indiana University Library. Additional information obtained by John G. Neihardt from the Hunkpapa, Iron Hawk, discloses that these soldiers "were so scared they didn't know what they were doing. They were making their arms go as though they were running very fast, but they were only walking. Some of them shot their guns in the air." See *Black Elk Speaks*, pp. 26-27.

that these men got considerable distance from the battlefield before being killed?

A. Does not know of any getting away.

Q. Were any of the wounded soldiers alive after the battle,
and what was done with them? Who killed them—the
squaws or the warriors?

A. Does not know of any. Saw squaws going up to where
soldiers lay, [and] he supposed [they went] to strip them.

Q. Were any soldiers taken to the village alive?

A. No, none were taken to the village.

Q. Why were none of the soldiers around Custer (at "G")
scalped?

A. Did not care to scalp any as they all had short hair. Did
not know Custer or his brother from anyone else.

Q. Was Custer (Long Hair) recognized during the fight or
afterward?

---

[8]The death of this soldier was witnessed by the Cheyenne, Wooden Leg, who claimed
that this individual was a suicide. In spite of the alleged reluctance of the Cheyennes to
touch such individuals, very little time was lost by one Cheyenne to remove the scalp of
this suicide and to display it. See Marquis, *Wooden Leg,* pp. 233-34. See also McCreight,
Firewater and Forked Tongues, p. 114, which may describe the same individual, although
in this case the victim was overtaken and killed by Crazy Horse. The location of this kill
site is known to battlefield personnel as Marker 174, which site yielded the following
artifacts during the survey of 1984: three spent 45/55 casings, one Colt revolver cartridge,
one Colt bullet which was vertically impacted into the ground, and one deformed 50/70
slug. Archeologists speculate that this individual was able to defend himself for a short
while with his carbine. However, subsequent pressure by the arriving Indians did not
allow him time to reload, whereupon he resorted to his revolver. He was apparently shot
while drawing his Colt because his convulsive reaction discharged the revolver into the
ground. See Scott and Fox, Jr., *Archaeological Insights into the Custer Battle,* p. 124.

[9]The statement about the man who ate frogs is corroborated by the Minneconjou,
Flying By. See Hammer, *Custer in '76,* p. 210. In regards to the alleged transfer of Tom
Custer's body, it may interest the reader to know that the Cheyennes may have outdone
the Sioux with an even more incredible tale. In their case it was told that they had carried
General Custer's body from the monument site all the way to Reno Hill, to deliver his
remains to the surviving troops. However, having been fired upon by Reno's soldiers,
they aborted any further attempts, but they were kind enough to return Custer's body to
the location where it was later found! See Marquis, *Custer on the Little Bighorn,* pp.
17-18.

A. Custer was not recognized.

Q. Was Tom Custer (Little Hair) recognized during the fight or after he was dead?

A. Tom Custer was not recognized.

Q. Was any scout recognized during the fight or after he was dead?

A. Did not know of any scout being recognized.

Q. How many Indians were killed or wounded?

A. Could not state how many were killed. Quite a number were wounded.

Q. How soon after the Custer battle did the Indians leave to attack the soldiers (Reno) on the bluff?

A. Right after the fight with Custer.

Q. Why were the Indians unable to kill Reno and his soldiers like they did to Custer's men?

A. An Indian courier came from down the river [and] brought news that Crook [Gen. Alfred H. Terry] was coming, and they made haste to get away.

Q. Was there any quarreling between Sitting Bull and Gall or any other chiefs during the night after the battle, and what about?

A. Never heard of any quarrel.

Q. Why were 30 dead Indians left in the village when the Indians left?

A. Heard that other soldiers were coming and did not take time to bury them.

Q. Who was the chief of [a:] the Blackfeet in the fight? Of [b:] the Minneconjous? Who was chief of [c:] the Sans Arcs (without a bow)? Who was chief of [d:] the Brule warriors?

A. A: did not know; b: Lame Deer and Spotted Elk; c: Spotted Eagle; d: Brules had no chief; they were a hunting party who fell in with this outfit at this point.

Q. Was American Horse, afterward killed at Slim Buttes, there and with what tribe?

A. American Horse was not there.

Q. When the Sioux fought Crook, where was the village? How far from the battle with Crook?

A. On the Rosebud, or rather a branch. [We] were fighting at long range. Village was about ready to move at the time of the fight.

Q. How many tepees were there in the village of your particular tribe?

A. Witness is not clear about the information on the tepees. There were some Arapahoes, [but] their tepees were scattered among the other bands and among relatives.

Q. Were any men killed in the deep gully at "H" [Deep Ravine]? How many—just a few or a good many?

A. There were quite a number killed in gully at "H", [but] not so many as at "G" [Custer Hill].

Q. When the soldiers arrived at "G", did many of them have their horses?

A. The most of the soldiers at "G" were afoot.

Q. How long did the battle at "G", last? If a long time, why so long? Did the soldiers there run out of ammunition before the Indians closed in on them?

A. They made a longer stand at "G" [Custer Hill] than at any other place. The warriors had the guns and ammunition of the soldiers at this time and were better equipped to fight. (And so would save their own ammunition—WMC.)

Q. Were there any defects in the guns?

A. No.

Q. Did the cartridges stick in the guns, and when shot off could the jacket be easily removed?

A. The guns were good.

Q. Did the soldiers who ran from "G" [Custer Hill] toward "H" [Deep Ravine] have their guns and ammunition?

A. A few had guns, [and] all had revolvers. Some of the men running away had revolvers in their belts that had never been used. All [soldiers] were in bad state for want of water.

Q. Were any of the soldiers seen to commit suicide or to shoot each other when finally surrounded?

A. Did not see anything of that kind.

THE BRULÉ LAKOTA, HOLLOW HORN BEAR (1850-1913)
This photo was probably taken by Heyn and Matzen of Omaha,
Nebraska, ca. 1900, when Hollow Horn Bear was about 50 years old.
This image was selected to appear on the 14 cent stamp issued in 1922.

Courtesy of National Anthropological Archives, Smithsonian Institution.

The Hollow Horn Bear
Interview

Editorial note: This interview was conducted in 1909 by Sewell B. Weston who based his inquiries on a quesionnaire submitted by Walter M. Camp. This interview resulted in three letter-size pages of text, containing 51 typed answers to questions. The manuscript further reveals three annotations in Camp's handwriting, and two notes on separate pages, also by Camp. The following is a verbatim transcript of the original manuscript, to which I have added Camp's questions.

Hollow Horn Bear
[Location not given]
June, 1909[1]

Q. Name and age and to what tribe did you belong?
A. Hollow Horn Bear (Mato Heli Dogeca), 59 years. Brule.
Q. Were you a hostile, or an agency Indian, and where had you spent the winter?

---

[1]Born in 1850, Hollow Horn Bear was the son of Iron Shell, a distinguished leader of the Orphan Band of the Brule Lakotas. It was said that the former was found by soldiers on the deserted battlefield of the Bluewater in Nebraska, where troops under General William S. Harney destroyed a small village of Brules on September 3, 1855. Hollow Horn Bear came from a large family, and although he was not the oldest son, he later succeeded his father as a tribal leader. He married Good Bed Woman, and after the surrender in 1876, he became known as a progressive leader who advocated the adoption

A. Agency [Indian]. At Spotted Tail Agency, on Beaver Creek.[2]

Q. What chief were you fighting under, and where did your tribe or band join Sitting Bull.

A. Buffalo Horse. Hollow Horn Bear had some horses that had either strayed or were stolen. He, in company with about 20 Two Kettle Indians, was out looking for these horses. While at Heart Creek, a branch of the Yellowstone, he first saw soldiers. This was in the latter part of May or the 1st of June. The Soldiers were headed westward. He states that he was informed that this was Custer's outfit. This bunch followed the soldiers for two days and then cut across to the Greasy Grass and joined Sitting Bull. (Heart River runs east, north of and parallel with the Cannon Ball. It empties into the Missouri. The headwaters of it are nearly over to the Little Missouri and right along Custer's line of march. This might have been the stream where Hollow Horn first saw Custer's troops—WMC.)[3]

Q. Were you in the fight against Crook's soldiers on the Rosebud a week before the fight with Custer?

A. No.

of the white man's way of life. See George E. Hyde, *Spotted Tail's Folk* (Norman, 1961), pp. 61, 264; Henry W. Hamilton and Jean Tyree Hamilton, *The Sioux of the Rosebud* (Norman, 1971), p. 176. The Hollow Horn Bear interview was conducted by Sewell B. Weston at the request of Walter M. Camp. It is contained in the Camp Collection, Custer Battlefield National Monument, National Park Service, and it is hereby reproduced with their permission.

[2] In 1876, Spotted Tail Agency, so named after the renowned chief of the Brules, was located in the northwest corner of Nebraska. In 1877, this agency was transferred to the Missouri River against the objections of the Brule people. However, the following year they were allowed to return and they relocated their present agency on Rosebud Creek, South Dakota. For an excellent study of the struggle of the Brules, see Hyde, *Spotted Tail's Folk.*

[3] The individual named Buffalo Horse has not been identified. Nick Ruleau told Ricker that the Brules were led by Flying Chaser, which is corroborated by the Oglala, He Dog, who added that the former was the head man, but not a big chief. See Hammer, *Custer in '76,* p. 206.

Q. How many days were you in the village before the Custer fight?

A. About 5 days.

Q. How many tepees or how many warriors were in the village of your own tribe?

A. About 65 tepees, and 30 warriors. (And a good many young bucks who qualified as warriors and [who] were not with the women—WMC.]

Q. How long before the fight was it learned that soldiers were coming?

A. Just shortly after the fight with Reno.

Q. What preparation was then made to meet the soldiers? Why did the Indians not go out several miles to meet the soldiers?

A. They were practically prepared to fight Custer. They went to Custer as soon as they could recover from the earlier fight with Reno. Some talk had to be indulged in before they went to Custer, which took some time.

Q. Did the Indians suppose it was Crook's soldiers or Custer's soldiers that were coming? Did the Indians expect to be attacked in the daytime?

A. Heard someone say that he saw a man with a red and yellow handkerchief around his neck and a buckskin jacket on. The warrior who made the remark said it must be Long Yellow Hair. Had no idea to offer relative to a night or day attack.[4]

Q. Were you in the first fighting, at the Hunkpapa tepees? State any noteworthy occurrence that you remember

---

[4]The Cheyennes reported a somewhat simular observation. They told Grinnell that this man was "clad in a buckskin shirt, fringed on the breast, with buckskin trousers; wore fine, high boots, and had a knife stuck in a scabbord in his boot. A large red handkerchief was tied about his neck.... He had a mustache, but no other hair on his face, and had blue marks pricked into the skin on the arms above the wrist." Grinnell commented that this was probably Tom Custer. See *The Fighting Cheyennes*, p. 353.

concerning this fight. Did the Indians all have their ponies when this fight started?

A. Yes. Was among the first to cross the river. Some of the young warriors rode back and forth in front of Custer's front before any real change was made. None of these were killed, a good omen that the Indians would win the day. Most of the Indians were mounted; a good many however, were afoot.

Q. How long after this first fight did soldiers appear opposite the village, and where was this second party of soldiers (Custer) first seen. (This is an important question, and I would give the witness plenty of time to answer it. Let him point out the place on the map without any suggestion from the questioner; or let him say whether Custer first appeared opposite some particular part of the village, such as the Minneconjou or Sans Arc tepees, or elsewhere.)

A. About one hour. Witness was at the Brule village and first saw the soldiers over the top of the high ridge at about "E" [Nye-Cartwright Ridge].

Q. How near the river did these soldiers come, and were they at any time near Ford "B"?

A. Custer got as far as the ridge south of "C" [bluff]. (As shown on the blueprint.) Never got any nearer to the river.[5]

Q. Did these soldiers fire across the river into the village before the fight started, and did they hit anyone in the village?

A. Yes, soldiers fired into the village, [but] no one was hit.

─────────────

[5]The ridge south of "C" is sometimes identified as Greasy Grass Hill. In actuality, it is the western terminus of Calhoun Ridge which geographical formation extends to the river. Initially, Greasy Grass Hill was held by troopers. Increased pressure by the Indians forced the survivors to abandon this position, leaving in their wake a number of dead and a quantity of expended military casings. Although only three markers have been placed at this location, evidence gathered by Walter Camp indicates that as many as eight soldiers may have died here. See Hardorff, *Markers, Artifacts and Indian Testimony*, pp. 41-42.

Q. Did the Indians cross the river and attack Custer's soldiers immediately, as soon as they appeared, or were the soldiers in sight over there a considerable time, and what did the soldiers appear to be doing?

A. Quite a little talk was indulged in before an attack was made on Custer after he was first seen.

Q. Did it appear that the soldiers were preparing to cross over and attack the village?

A. They did not appear to want to cross after the warriors made their presence felt in such large numbers.

Q. Did the fight start near the river or back on the ridge where the soldiers were finally all killed?

A. The fight started somewhere near the ridge south of "C" as shown on blueprint.

Q. If the fighting started near the river, was there heavy fighting as the soldiers fell back to the ridge, and were the soldiers all together, in one body, or were there two widely separated parties of them?

A. The fighting was heavy at the start. Soldiers gave ground from the start. In the early start of fight, soldiers in front were dismounted and many of their horses were killed. There was no fighting near the river.

Q. In falling back from the river, did the soldiers go by way of "H" and "G", or by way of "C" and "D". In other words, were the soldiers lying between "H" and "G" killed in the first fighting or in the last part of it?

A. Soldiers went from "C" [bluff] to "D" [Calhoun Hill]. Those killed between "H" [Deep Ravine] and "G" [Custer Hill] was at last of fight.

Q. After the soldiers got to the ridge, did they keep together in one body, or did some of them make a stand to give the others a chance to select a position?

A. Soldiers kept together all during the fight. The soldiers would shift positions, [but] no stand [was] being made to do so.

Q. Was a determined stand made at any of the points "C", "D" or "K" by part of the soldiers, or were all of the soldiers together at these different points, and were they trying to hold their ground or were they moving?

A. The soldiers kept moving all the time. Witness states that the soldiers were drunk. (Demoralized.)

Q. If no stand was made at "K", how came there to be so many men killed there in a bunch?

A. By the time the soldiers got to "K" many of the warriors had the guns and ammunition of dead soldiers. Many of the soldiers at this point tried to get off the top of the ridge and make their escape, and [they] got in a pocket, or trap, where they were easily killed. (That is, they came from Calhoun's position to low ground where Indians were thickly massed in gully—WMC.)

Q. (Important!) Did you see any considerable number of soldiers holding horses for dismounted men at any time during the fight, and where was this? (Let him point it out on the map.) Or did all of the men, individually, take care of their own horses?

A. The only time was when the soldiers made the stand nearest to the village. Some of the mounted men held the horses for those who were dismonted.[6]

Q. (Important!) At any time during the fight were the men strung out at intervals in good order, in a long line as between "C" and "D", or between "D" and "K", or between "K" and "G", or did they keep pretty much together all the time?

---

[6]This observation is confirmed by Moving Robe Woman who noticed these horseholders on Calhoun Ridge immediately after she crossed the river.

A. At the start of the fight the soldiers were in good order, but soon after they became demoralized. By the time "C" was reached they were bunched.

Q. How can we explain the men scattered along in the direct line between "C" [bluff] and "H" [Deep Ravine]? How came they to be killed? It looks like a line had been formed to fight there.

A. [In] reference to these men, [witness] cannot state [anything] as he was on opposite side of the ridge. These men probably tried to get away at the last of the fight. (This was probably the fact—WMC.) (Thunder Hawk's squaw thinks these men were dragged there.)[7]

Q. The men killed between "H" and "G", were they standing in line or were they running, and which way were they running? Did they have guns and ammunition?

A. Could not state as he was [not] in a position to see.

Q. What did you see of the men killed in the deep gully?

A. Same answer as above.

Q. In the last stand at "G", did the soldiers appear to run short of ammunition?

A. No. They fought as hard at "G" as at any other point.

Q. Were the soldiers here all shot down at long range, or was there fighting at close quarters at the last of the fight?

A. The fighting was at close quarters. This witness used his war club at this point.

Q. Did many of the soldiers at "G" have horses and did they keep them long?

A. Nearly all had horses.

Q. Assuming that some of the soldiers broke from this point and tried to get away, were any of them mounted?

---

[7] For information on Thunder Hawk and his wife, see the interview with Julia Face hereafter.

A. He did not see at any time any of the soldiers make a rush to get away. Said they were all brave men.

Q. How long did the fight last where the last stand was made at "G"?

A. Just a few minutes. (Witness could not tell whether one or ten.)

Q. At what part of the battlefield were you stationed, or at what particular points do you remember being at?

A. [He] was on the opposite side of the ridge from river, all the way around from "C" [bluff] to "G" [Custer Hill]. At all points except at "H".

Q. What did you see of the company having gray horses? Did they keep together? At what point particularly did you see the gray horses?

A. Saw gray horses from the first. They kept fairly well together. Some of the soldiers on these horses were in the last of the fight.

Q. At any time during the fight did the soldiers make a charge and where was this, if they did so?

A. Soldiers never made a charge.

Q. Were many of the horses captured early in the fight?

A. Horses were captured soon after the fight commenced. Could not state how many.

Q. While the soldiers were being killed at "K" [Keogh's stand], where were the Indians? Were they in gully north of "K", or were they on the ridge just south of "K" as well as in the gully?

A. The warriors seemed to him to be in their own way at this point. He did not stop here.

Q. Where did the soldiers seem to fight the hardest?

A. The hardest fight was at the start.

Q. Was any ammunition found on the dead soldiers at "G" [Custer Hill]?

A. Soldiers at "G" had plenty of ammunition.

Q. Were any of the wounded soldiers permitted to live long after the fight?

A. Could not answer.

Q. Why were so few of the soldiers scalped at point "G"?

A. Hair was too short.

Q. Was Custer (Long Hair) recognized on the battlefield, dead or alive?

A. Heard someone say that he saw a man with a red and yellow handkerchief around his neck and a buckskin jacket on. The warrior who made this remark said it must be Long Yellow Hair.

Q. When was it first known to the Indians that Custer had been killed?

A. Some time before [it was] generally known. [Who said Indians did not have a sense of humor?!—RGH.]

Q. Did you ever hear how many Indians were killed altogether, in all of the tribes of the village or how many wounded altogether?

A. Six killed and six wounded; the latter all recovered.[8]

Q. In the two day's fighting against Reno on the bluff, four miles from the Custer fight, why were so many Indians not able to defeat the soldiers there also?

A. Reno had burrowed in the ground like a prairie dog. Guns and arrows could not reach him.

Q. Did many or most of the Indians have Winchester rifles (pump guns)?

A. What guns the Indians had were Winchester carbines.

---

[8]The dead count of the Indians amounted to some forty people, none of whom were reported to be Brules.

As fast as the soldiers were killed, the Indians would take their arms and ammunition.

Q. Why did the Indians quit Reno and move the village on the second day?

A. Indians were all in as far as the fighting was concerned. They had got enough.

Q. When the Indians took up the village and moved out of the valley, did they still have plenty of ammunition?

A. Yes, were extra well supplied. Many carried two rifles.

Q. When the Indians moved they left a tepee in the village in which there were seven or eight dead Indians finely robed and tied in standing positions surrounding a center pole or post. What significance had this, if any? Were any of the dead Indians left in the village for want of means of transportation to carry them away?

A. The dressing of the Indians in this way was done to show proper respect to the dear departed. Sioux on the warpath never bury dead.

Q. Had any of the Indians killed in the Crook fight been brought to this village?

A. Did not know of any.

Q. After moving the village from the valley, how long did the seven tribes keep together, and where did they go?

A. Started for the Mt (Big Horn). Afterwards concluded it was not a good place. [We] turned and came down the Tongue River. After going along that some distance the tribes split up, the larger band continuing on down the river.

Q. Did any soldier break out of the Custer Fight and get a considerable distance away, mounted or dismounted, and how was he overtaken and killed?

A. Does not know of any.

The Julia Face Interview

Editorial note: This interview was conducted in 1909 by Sewell B. Weston who based his inquiries on a questionnaire submitted by Walter M. Camp. This interview resulted in two letter-size pages of text, containing 32 typed answers to questions, and one notation in Camp's handwriting. The following is a verbatim transcript of the original manuscript, to which I have added Camp's questions.

Julia Face
[Location not given]
June, 1909[1]

Q. How old is witness?
A. 51 years. (Proper name [is] Julia Face.)
Q. With what tribe of Sioux was she at the time of the

---

[1] Born in 1858, Julia Face was the daughter of a head soldier of the Oglala Lakotas named Face. She was the wife of the Brule, Thunder Hawk, and as such she became known to Sewell B. Weston who interviewed her at the request of Walter M. Camp. Her statement is identified as the *Interview with Thunder Hawk's Squaw,* which is contained in the Walter Camp Collection, Custer National Monument, National Park Service. The interview is hereby reproduced with their permission. The Camp Collection at Bringham Young University Library contains several letters from Sewell to Camp regarding the credibility of Julia's statements. Thunder Hawk's short account of the Custer Battle was retold by A.G. Shaw to Eli S. Ricker in 1909, and it is contained in the Ricker Collection, reel 3, tablet 11, Nebraska State Historical Society.

battle? Who was the fighting chief of the tribe at the battle?

A. With Oglalas. Crazy Horse.

Q. Was witness in fight with Crook on the Rosebud 8 days previous to Custer battle, and what way did trail lead to Greasy Grass Creek?

A. Yes. Followed numerous dry creeks and draws in about as a direct line from Rosebud to Greasy Grass as possible.

Q. How many days were you in the village before the Custer fight?

A. Had just arrived the night before.

Q. When did Indian scouts first bring news of the approach of soldiers, and did they suppose them to be Crook or Custer.

A. Can not state. The soldiers were down as near to the camp as they ever got when she was first apprised of any being near. (In explanation will state that her husband was in the tepee suffering from a wound in the left hip he received on the Rosebud, and she was caring for him. She had been in the hills just prior to this where she went during the Reno fight. As the wound was giving her husband much trouble, she was practically oblivious to everything else until the warriors turned out en masse to go after Custer.)[2]

Q. What part of the village or what tepees did soldiers charge first?

A. They seemed to be shooting into the Sans Arcs, Minneconjous and Oglalas.[3]

Q. And what part of the village did the soldiers next appear, and how near did they get to the village?

---

[2]Thunder Hawk had two wives who both attended to him during the battle of the Little Bighorn. Around the turn of the century, this Brule committed a capital offense, causing him to be imprisoned at Hot Springs, South Dakota, where he suicided.

[3]Although the question has reference to Reno's charge, the answer indicated that the informant referred to Custer's approach.

A. They never charged any part of the village. About a half mile.

Q. How long after the first fight did soldiers appear opposite the village, and where was this second party of soldiers (Custer's) first seen?

A. About two hours. Custer was first seen at a point between the Blackfeet and the Sans Arcs.

Q. How many tepees or how many warriors were there in the village of your own tribe?

A. A great many. (Oglalas.)

Q. Was the village surprised, and did squaws prepare to leave?

A. Yes. Squaws and children left the village. Some of them went a considerable distance.

Q. Was there considerable fighting at this point, and what caused Custer to go from there to the high ridge where he was killed?

A. At the start there was considerable fighting done. [She] thinks there were so many warriors that Custer was looking for a place to get where he could fight to a better advantage.

Q. Did the Indians reach the high ridge ahead of Custer, and did he at any time charge them and drive them off?

A. None of the warriors reached the high ridge ahead of Custer. The Indians acted just like they were driving buffalo to a good place where they could be easily slaughtered. Custer never charged.

Q. Custer's men lay killed and strung out over a line about 1¼ miles long, in the shape of a letter U with open ends toward creek. Now, was a stand made at one place or at several places? If made at only one place, then most of the men must have been killed running, were they not?

A. No stand of any duration was made. (Witness was quite a ways from the battle, being at the Oglala tepees. She had a good view from that distance.) Soldiers were killed [while] moving.

Q. Did the soldiers fire across the river into the village before the fight started, and did they hit anyone in the village?

A. Witness did not hear any shooting until the warriors started out to fight Custer. Then the shooting seemed to be confined to the Sans Arc, Minneconjou and Oglala tepees. (These are probably those who attacked Custer first—WMC.)

Q. At what point on the map were the last soldiers killed, and were they on foot or on horses?

A. At "H" [Deep Ravine]. There was a soldier, mounted, who tried to get away. He turned to retrace along the ridge. This was the last able soldier that she saw alive. The soldiers at "H" [Deep Ravine] were partly mounted and partly afoot, the preponderence mounted.

Q. What part of the battle did witness see?

A. Practically all, except at "K" [Keogh's stand] when many of the soldiers were out of sight. Witness states that the dead soldiers were quite plain as the Indians would strip them and their skins would shine in the sunlight. They would rob the soldiers and take their money and keep the silver and gold [coins], but would throw the paper money away.

Q. Did any man escape to the river?

A. No soldiers reached the river.

Q. Was Long Yellow Hair (Custer) recognized in the fight or among the dead on day of battle?

A. No one recognized Custer. It was thought he was some cowboy.

Q. How soon after the battle was witness on the ground?

A. Witness started to the battlefield. After going about halfway [she] turned and went back to her husband.

Q. Were any of the wounded soldiers still alive, and how were they killed?

A. Witness did not get near enough to make a personal investigation.

Q. Were many of the soldiers scalped, and if not, why not?

A. None were scalped—hair was too short.

Q. In falling back from the river, did the soldiers go by way of "H" and "G", or by way of "C" and "D". In other words, were the soldiers lying between "H" and "G" killed in the first of the fight, or at the last part of it?

A. Soldiers went from "C" [bluff] to "D" [Calhoun Hill] and on to "H" [Deep Ravine] via "K" [Keogh's stand].

Q. After the soldiers got to the ridge, did they keep together in one body, or did some of them make a stand to give others a chance to select a position?

A. The soldiers were all together when they reached the top of the ridge. By this time they were surrounded on the sides and in the rear.

Q. At what stage of the battle were any cavalry horses captured, and was there considerable ammunition on them?

A. A great many horses were brought into camp after the fight. [She] could not state as to the amount of ammunition that was in the saddlebags.

Q. Was Chief American Horse in this battle and with what tribe?

A. No. American Horse was not there.

Q. How many Indians were killed?

A. Could not answer. Witness had a brother-in-law killed.

Q. Were any of the wounded soldiers taken into the village and tortured?

A. No wounded or other soldiers were taken to the village.

Q. How long did the fight last where the last stand was made at "G"?

A. Could not state just how long a stand was made here. Quite a fight was made at this point.

Q. When was it first known to the Indians that Custer was killed?

A. That same night it was rumored that it was Custer. Some little time after it was confirmed.

Q. Had any of the Indians killed in the Crook fight been brought to this village?

A. Plenty Lice and another warrior were wounded on the Rosebud. [They] died in the camp on the Greasy Grass.[4]

---

[4]Since Julia Face was a member of her father's Oglala band, she probably would have had knowledge of the Oglala casualties sustained during the Rosebud Battle. However, in spite of his wound, it seems that the Oglala, Plenty Lice, partook in the battle at the Little Bighorn because several Lakota sources reported him slain on Custer's battlefield. See, for example, Hammer, *Custer in '76*, p. 267.

Bibliography
and Index

Bibliography

ARCHIVAL SOURCES

Billings, Montana. Billings Public Library. Billings Clipping File.

Bloomington, Indiana. University of Indiana Library. Manuscripts Division. Robert S. Ellison Collection: Walter M. Camp Manuscripts.

Columbia, Missouri. University of Missouri Library and Missouri Historical Society. Joint Collection. Western History Manuscripts Collection: John G. Neihardt Collection.

Crow Agency, Montana. Custer Battlefield National Monument. Walter M. Camp Collection. Elizabeth B. Custer Collection.

Denver, Colorado. Denver Public Library. Western History Division. Robert S. Ellison Collection: Walter Mason Camp Papers.

Laramie, Wyoming. University of Wyoming Library. Western History Research Center. Special Collections: Agnes W. Spring Collection.

Lincoln, Nebraska. Nebraska State Historical Society. Eli S. Ricker Collection.

New York. New York Public Library. Manuscripts Division: Francis R. Hagner Collection.

Norman, Oklahoma. University of Oklahoma Library. Western History Collection: Walter S. Campbell Collection

Pierre, South Dakota. South Dakota Historical Resource Center. Manuscripts Division: James McLaughlin Letter.

Provo, Utah. Brigham Young University Library. Manuscripts Division: Walter Mason Camp Manuscripts.

Washington, D.C. Smithsonian Institution. National Anthropological Archives: Hugh L. Scott Collection.

PRINTED SOURCES

Books

Berthrong, Donald J. *The Southern Cheyennes.* Norman: University of Oklahoma Press, 1963.

Blish, Helen H. *A Pictographic History of the Oglala Sioux.* Lincoln: University of Nebraska Press, 1967.

Bourke, John G. *On the Border with Crook.* New York: Charles Scribner's, 1891.

Boyes, William. *Custer's Black White Man.* Washington, D.C.: South Capitol Press, 1972.

Brown, Mark H. and W.R. Felton. *The Frontier Years: L.A. Huffman, Photographer of the Plains.* New York: Henry Holt, 1955.

Burdick, Usher L. *Tales from the Buffalo Land.* Baltimore: Wirth Brothers, 1940.

———. *David F. Barry's Indian Notes on the Custer Battle.* Baltimore: Wirth Brothers, 1949.

Carroll, John M. *The Benteen-Goldin Letters on Custer and His Last Battle.* New York: Liveright, 1974.

———. *The Arrest and Killing of Sitting Bull: A Documentary.* Glendale, Calif.: Arthur H. Clark Co., 1987.

Chandler, Melbourne C. *Of Garry Owen in Glory: The History of the Seventh United States Cavalry Regiment.* Annandale, Calif.: privately printed, 1960.

Crawford, Lewis F. *Rekindling Camp Fires: The Exploits of Ben Arnold.* Bismark, N. Dak.: Capitol Book Co., 1926.

Curtis, Edward S. *The North American Indians* III. Cambridge: The University Press, 1908.

Custer, George A. *My Life on the Plains.* Lincoln: University of Nebraska Press, 1966.

DeBarthe, Joe. *Life and Adventures of Frank Grouard.* Norman: University of Oklahoma Press, 1958.

DeMallie, Raymond J., ed., *The Sixth Grandfather: Black Elk's Teaching Given to John G. Neihardt.* Lincoln: University of Nebraska Press, 1984.

DeWall, Rob. *The Saga of Sitting Bull's Bones.* Crazy Horse, S. Dak.: Korczak's Heritage, Inc., 1984.

Dixon, Joseph K. *The Vanishing Race.* New York: Bonanza Books, 1975.

Finerty, John F. *War-path and Bivouac, or the Conquest of the Sioux.* Norman: University of Oklahoma Press, 1961.

Friswold, Carroll, comp. and Robert A. Clark, ed. *The Killing of Chief Crazy Horse.* Glendale, Calif.: Arthur H. Clark Co., 1976.

Graham, W.A. *The Custer Myth: A Source Book of Custeriana.* New York: Bonanza Books, 1953.

———. *Abstract of the Official Record of the Reno Court of Inquiry.* Harrisburg: Stackpole, 1954.

Gray, John S. *Centennial Campaign: The Sioux War of 1876.* Fort Collins, Colo.: Old Army Press, 1976.

Greene, Jerome A. *Slim Buttes, 1876: An Episode of the Great Sioux War.* Norman: University of Oklahoma Press, 1982.

Grinnell, George Bird. *The Fighting Cheyennes.* Norman: University of Oklahoma Press, 1956.

———. *The Cheyenne Indians.* 2 vols. Lincoln: University of Nebraska Press, 1972.

Hafen. LeRoy R. and Francis Marion Young. *Fort Laramie and the Pageant of the West,* 1834-1890. Lincoln: University of Nebraska Press, 1984.

Hammer, Kenneth. *Men with Custer.* Fort Collins, Colo.: Old Army Press, 1972.

———. ed. *Custer in '76: Walter Camp's Notes on e Custer Fight.* Provo: Brigham Young University Press, 1976.

Hardorff, Richard G. *The Oglala Lakota Crazy Horse: A Preliminary Genealogical Study and an Annotated Listing of Primary Sources.* Mattituck, N.Y.: J.M. Carroll Company, 1985.

———. *Markers, Artifacts and Indian Testimony: Preliminary Findings on the Custer Battle.* Short Hills, N.J.: Don Horn Publications, 1985.

———. *The Custer Battle Casualties: Burials, Exhumations and Reinterments.* El Segundo, Calif.: Upton & Sons, Publishers, 1989.

Hassrick, Royal B. *The Sioux: Life and Customs of a Warrior Society.* Norman: University of Oklahoma Press, 1964.

Howard, James H., trans. and ed. *The Warrior Who Killed Custer: The Personal Narrative of Chief Joseph White Bull.* Lincoln: University of Nebraska Press. 1968.

Hyde, George E. *Red Cloud's Folk: A History of the Oglala Sioux Indians.* Norman: University of Oklahoma Press, 1937.

————. *Life of George Bent.* Norman: University of Oklahoma Press, 1968.

Innes, Ben. *Bloody Knife!* Fort Collins, Colo.: Old Army Press, 1973.

Kuhlman, Charles. *Legend into History.* Fort Collins, Colo.: Old Army Press, 1977.

Libby, Orin G., ed. *The Arikara Narrative of the Campaign Against the Hostile Dakotas, June, 1876.* New York: Sol Lewis, 1973.

Magnussen, Daniel O. *Peter Thompson's Narrative of the Little Bighorn Campaign, 1876.* Glendale, Calif.: Arthur H. Clark Co., 1974.

Maine, Floyd Shuster. *Lone Eagle . . . The White Sioux.* Albuquerque: University of New Mexico Press, 1956.

Marquis, Thomas B. *Wooden Leg.* Lincoln: University of Nebraska Press, 1962.

————. *Custer on the Little Bighorn.* Lodi, Calif.: End-Kian Publishing, 1971.

————. *Cheyennes and Sioux.* Stockton, Calif.: University of the Pacific Press, 1973.

————. *Keep the Last Bullet for Yourself.* New York City: Two Continents Publishing Co., 1976.

Masters, Joseph G. *Shadows Fall Across the Little Horn: Custer's Last Stand.* Laramie: University of Wyoming Press, 1951.

McClernand, Edward J. *With the Indian and the Buffalo in Montana, 1870-1878.* Glendale, Calif.: Arthur H. Clark Co., 1969.

McCreight, M.I. *Firewater and Forked Tongues.* Pasadena, Calif.: Trail's End, 1947.

McLaughlin, James. *My Friend the Indian.* Seattle: Superior Publishing, 1970.

Miles, Nelson A. *Personal Recollections and Observations of General Nelson A. Miles.* New York: Werner Co., 1897.

Milligan, Edward A. *High Noon on the Greasy Grass.* Bottineau, N. Dak.: Bottineau Courant, 1972.

Mills, Charles K. *Harvest of Barren Regrets: The Army Career of Frederick William Benteen, 1834-1898.* Glendale, Calif.: Arthur H. Clark Co., 1985.

Neihardt, John G. *When the Tree Flowered: An Authentic Tale of the Old Sioux World.* New York: Macmillan, 1951.

_____. *Black Elk Speaks.* Lincoln: University of Nebraska Press, 1961.

Olson, James C. *Red Cloud and the Sioux Problem.* Lincoln: University of Nebraska Press, 1965.

Sandoz Mari. *Crazy Horse: The Strange Man of the Ogalalas.* Lincoln: University of Nebraska Press, 1961.

Scott, Douglass D. and Richard A. Fox, Jr. *Archaeological Insights into the Custer Battle.* Norman: University of Oklahoma Press, 1987.

Smith, DeCost. *Indian Experiences.* Caldwell, Idaho: Caxton Printers, 1943.

Stewart, Edgar I. *Custer's Luck.* Norman: University of Oklahoma Press, 1955

Standing Bear, Luther. *My People the Sioux.* Lincoln: University of Nebraska Press, 1975.

Stands in Timber, John and Margot Liberty. *Cheyenne Memories.* Lincoln: University of Nebraska Press, 1972.

Tassin, Ray. *Stanley Vestal, Champion of the Old West.* Glendale, Calif.: Arthur H. Clark Co., 1973.

Terrell, John Upton and George Walton. *Faint the Trumpet Sounds.* New York: David McKay, 1966.

Utley, Robert M., intro. *The Reno Court of Inquiry: The Chicago Times Account.* Fort Collins, Colo.: Old Army Press, 1972.

Vaughn, J.W. *With Crook at the Rosebud.* Harrisburg, Pa.: Stackpole, 1956.

_____. *The Reynolds Campaign on Powder River.* Norman: University of Oklahoma Press, 1961.

_____. *Indian Fights.* Norman: University of Oklahoma Press, 1966.

Vestal Stanley. *Sitting Bull, Champion of The Sioux.* Boston: Houghton Mifflin, 1932.

_____. *Warpath: The True Story of the Fighting Sioux Told in a Biography of Chief White Bull.* Boston: Houghton Mifflin, 1934.

_____. *New Sources of Indian History, 1850-1891.* Norman: University of Oklahoma Press, 1934.

_____. *Warpath and Council Fire.* New York: Random House, 1948.

Walker, Judson Elliott. *Campaigns of General Custer.* New York: Promontory Press, 1966.

Weibert, Henry and Don. *Sixty-six Years in Custer's Shadow.* Billings, Montana: Falcon Press, 1985.

Wheeler, Col. Homer W. *Buffalo Days.* Indianapolis: Bobbs-Merrill, 1925.

Yost, Nelly Snyder. *Boss Cowman: The Recollections of Ed Lemmon, 1857-1946.* Lincoln: University of Nebraska Press, 1969.

Articles

Anderson, Harry H. "Cheyennes at the Little Big Horn: A Study of Statistics." *North Dakota History* (Spring, 1960).

_____. "Indian Peace-Talkers and the Conclusion of the Sioux War of 1876." *Nebraska History* (December, 1963).

Baily, Edward C. "Echoes from Custer's Last Fight." *Military Affairs* (Winter, 1953).

Bradley, Lt. James H. "The Journal of." *Contributions to the Historical Society of Montana* II (1896).

Deland, Charles E. "The Sioux Wars." *South Dakota Historical Collections* XV (1930).

Eastman, Charles H. "The Story of the Little Big Horn." *Chautauquan* (July, 1900).

_____. "Rain-in-the-Face." *The Outlook* (October 27, 1906).

Garland, Hamlin. "General Custers Last Fight as Seen by Two Moons." *McClure Magazine* (September, 1898).

Gibbon, John "Last Summer's Expedition against the Sioux." *American Catholic Quarterly Review* (April, 1877).

Godfrey, Edward S. "Custer's Last Battle." *Century Magazine* (January, 1892).

Graham, W.A. "Custer's Battle Flags." *The Westerners Brand Book, 1950.* Los Angeles Westerners, 1951.

Gray, John S. "Arikara Scouts with Custer." *North Dakota History* (Spring, 1968).

Greene, Jerome A. "Evidence and the Custer Enigma: A Reconstruction of Indian-Military History." *The Westerners Trail Guide* (Kansas City) (March-June, 1973).

———. "The Lame Deer Fight: Last Drama of the Sioux War of 1876-1877." *By Valor and Arms* (Number 3, 1978).

Hardorff, Richard G. "Captain Keogh's Insurance Policy." *Research Review* (September, 1977).

———. "Custer's Trail to Wolf Mountains: A Reevaluation of Evidence." *Custer and His Times: Book Two.* Fort Worth: Little Bighorn Associates, 1984.

———. "The Frank Grouard Genealogy." *Custer and His Times: Book Two.* Fort Worth: Little Bighorn Associates, 1984.

Hedren, Paul L. "Carbine Extraction Failure at the Little Big Horn: A New Examination." *Military Collector and Historian* (Summer, 1973).

Knight, Oliver. "War or Peace: The Anxious Wait for Crazy Horse." *Nebraska History* (Winter, 1973).

Marshall, Robert A. "How Many Indians Were There?" *Research Review* (June, 1977).

Roe, Charles F. "The Custer Massacre: Narrative of Curley." *Army and Navy Journal* (March 25, 1882).

Stewart, Edgar I. "Which Indian Killed Custer?" *Montana: the Magazine of Western History* (Summer, 1958).

Vestal, Stanley. "White Bull and One Bull—An Appreciation." *Westerners Brand Book* (Chicago) (October, 1947).

———. "The Man Who Killed Custer." *American Heritage* (February, 1957).

Newspapers

Billings (Montana) *Daily Gazette,* 1911.

Billings Gazette, 1961

Bismarck (North Dakota) *Tribune,* 1876, and 1966

Chicago Daily Tribune, 1879

Hardin (Montana) *Tribune,* 1923

St. Paul Pioneer Press, 1886

Index

CPSIA information can be obtained
at www.ICGtesting.com
Printed in the USA
LVHW082246040921
696994LV00020B/476